ITHELL COLQUHOUN (1906–1988) was a painter and writer whose works contributed greatly to the British surrealist movement before and after the Second World War, and her phantasmagorical landscapes and penetrating portraits hang on the walls of major galleries across Britain. The daughter of a civil servant in India, Colquhoun was born in Assam in 1906, but was soon returned to England. She studied at Cheltenham Art School and the Slade School of Art, after which she took studios around Europe where she met, and was heavily influenced by, Paul Vézelay and André Breton. In 1942 she married fellow surrealist Toni del Renzio. An acrimonious divorce in 1947 also saw Colquhoun informally separate from the surrealist movement, leaving her free to explore her interest in mysticism, the esoteric and the occult. The results of this preoccupation are most evident in her writing, which includes the short novel *Goose of Hermogenes* (1961) and her two earlier travelogues, *The Crying of the Wind* (1955) and *The Living Stones* (1957). She died in Lamorna, Cornwall, in 1988.

STEWART LEE is a stand-up comedian and writer. He was born in 1968. His work includes *Jerry Springer: The Opera* and the BBC series *Stewart Lee's Comedy Vehicle*. His North London home is full of records and books.

Lough Inagh, Connemara

It is death to mock a poet
to love a poet
to be a poet.
— *Irish Triad*

THE
CRYING
OF THE WIND
Ireland

**By the same author
and published by Peter Owen**

Goose of Hermogenes

The Living Stones: Cornwall

The Crying
of the Wind
Ireland

Ithell Colquhoun

PETER OWEN
LONDON AND CHICAGO

PETER OWEN PUBLISHERS
Conway Hall, 25 Red Lion Square, London WC1R 4RL

Peter Owen books are distributed in the USA and Canada by
Independent Publishers Group/Trafalgar Square
814 North Franklin Street, Chicago, IL 60610, USA

First published in Great Britain 1954 by
Peter Owen Publishers
This edition 2016
Reprinted 2017 (twice)

PAPERBACK ISBN 978-0-7206-1894-5
EPUB ISBN 978-0-7206-1895-2
MOBIPOCKET ISBN 978-0-7206-1896-9
PDF ISBN 978-0-7206-1897-6

A catalogue record for this book is available
from the British Library

Printed by CPI (UK) Ltd, Croydon, CR0 4YY

Contents

Photographs

All photographs credited to Capt Seumas MacCall

A NOTE ON SPELLINGS

In this reprint edition we have retained, for the most part, the author's spellings of Irish place-names and words and passages from Gaelic. There are some exceptions – loch has been changed to lough, Glendaloch to Glendalough, Grainne to Gráinne, the goddess Eiré to Ériu, for instance – but otherwise we have not attempted to update or standardize the text and have left most of it as Ithell Colquhoun originally wrote.

Foreword

Ithell Colquhoun – Your Gnostic Travel Guide, Now and Always

The Crying of the Wind (1955), though purportedly a book about a journey around Ireland, is the experimental novel the surrealist artist and occult biographer Ithell Colquhoun never knew she had written; and its more self-aware successor, the 1957 account of her life in Cornwall's Penwith peninsula, *The Living Stones*, may yet work a magical transformation on your relationship with any landscape around you.

Both books are now impossibly expensive in their legendarily scarce original editions, and both were many decades out of print until now. How I envy you if you are about to read either, or both, of Ithell Colquhoun's gnostic travelogues for the first time, for soon you, too, will be post-Colquhoun, and everything will seem ever so slightly altered.

Born in British India in 1906, Colquhoun is best known as a surrealist painter and, latterly, as an occultist, eventually writing a difficult allegorical novel influenced by her interests, entitled *Goose of Hermogenes*, and a biography, *Sword of Wisdom*, of the would-be Hackney magus Samuel Liddell MacGregor Mathers, who was born a few minutes' walk from the kitchen table where I first began writing this introduction.

If you've ever wandered the aisles of the Royal Cornwall Museum, the Southampton Art Gallery or the Victoria and Albert Museum, you're probably aware of Colquhoun's art without realizing it and would find her better-known paintings strangely familiar. I scour auction sites online, repeatedly missing the affordable ones by mere months.

I assume I must have picked up *The Living Stones*, and my first-edition copy of the book's predecessor *The Crying of the Wind*, in now-long-gone bookshops somewhere in the 1990s, far from home, away doing stand-up comedy shows.

Their author-etched archaeological drawings and cryptically vague titles probably meant they looked to me, in my intuitive ignorance, as if they fitted the longstanding folk-mystic second-hand book bender I'm still on. They must have cost less than a fiver apiece, too, or I'd have passed on them in my youthful frugality. And then they probably sat unread, on shelves full of other good intentions, for years before I tackled them, unaware of the treasure within.

I know, however, that I had definitely read my ex-Torquay Public Library first edition of *The Living Stones* by the middle of 2007. Of this I am certain, because later that year we were on a sudden summer holiday with our five-month-old firstborn in a rented net loft in Mousehole, and the faerie voice of Ithell Colquhoun bustled at me from the hedgerows all week. My new wife became bored with me repeatedly quoting fact and opinion from *The Living Stones*, as it dawned on her what a tiresome man she was now shackled to.

Colquhoun had journeyed to her new home in the post-war wilderness of West Cornwall alone, charmed the suspicious natives, carved out her patch of ground, decoded the folk customs and sacred symbols around her and recorded her experiences. And in that Cornish Indian summer, for me, the stories within *The Living Stones* lived again.

The Mousehole house called the Lobster Pot, for example, that Colquhoun's much admired 'great beast' Aleister Crowley had briefly occupied, was still there; and the branches of the trees that vaulted the once largely untravelled lane down to Lamorna Cove, alongside which Colquhoun had dwelt alone in her Spartan Vow Cave studio, were reshaped now by the daily battering of motor vehicles, whose increasingly detrimental effects she had noted in 1957 with prophetic environmental anxiety.

The mass-marketed metal images of a lucky Cornish pixie – based on a witch called Joan the Wad – which had amused Colquhoun had become ubiquitous, and we recognized the ongoing monetization of supposedly antique authenticity all around us in souvenir shops; and when I remembered how her Lamorna idyll was interrupted by newfangled radio noise, Colquhoun worrying that technological opportunities for 'indiscriminate listening' would render us incapable of appreciating anything, I wondered what she would make of the backpackers' mobile phones that buzzed even within earshot of the sacred rocks of Mên-an-Tol, interrupting my intended reverie.

And when I told my wife of how Colquhoun, too, had been unconvinced by Tintagel's gauche attempts to turn the gaseous King Arthur myth into solid financial reality, she smiled a little at least, as we stood, like our spirit guide half a century before us, admiring mock-historic portraiture in the 'debased Victorian academic style' beneath the opportunistic 1930s arches of the ersatz King Arthur's Hall.

Meanwhile, all along the moors, standing in circles or pointing skywards, the living stones themselves lay largely intact half a century later, monuments to man's eternal need, as exemplified by Colquhoun in all her endeavours, to make artistic, philosophical and magical sense of our environment.

Colquhoun's time-travelling survey of Cornwall's culture and history brings ghosts and dead landscapes to life all around you, doing for the westernmost county what Arthur Machen did for London, what Alan Moore does for Northampton and what Frank Waters did for the American South-West.

And, like Machen lamenting the London of literary legend he arrived too late to live through, and Johnson and Boswell regretting the real Highlands that they missed by mere decades, Colquhoun senses the land she loves is fading.

'It seemed that my way home was marked out by ancient stones,' she writes, as she approaches the book's final chapter. And there we meet Albert Mellor, a pedlar who never learned to read or write, a soon-to-disappear denizen of Lamorna's 'vanishing seclusion'. For the woodland thins, 'Marauders have come with saws', laments Colquhoun, 'and raided the land for firewood.'

Though a superficially similar catalogue of traveller's tales and historical and geographical observations, *The Crying of the Wind* is a very different book to its successor, *The Living Stones*. Where *The Living Stones* begins with an explicit treatise, Colquhoun aquaplaning through snake worship, Atlantean myth and saints' feast-days to declaim a unified theory of human apprehension of the landscape, *The Crying of the Wind* begins poetically with a description of a ruined Irish manor and its decrepit owners that we are left to respond to as we see fit and which sets the tone for the stark contrasts between the two works.

The Living Stones is weighty with detail and qualification, but the earlier *The Crying of the Wind* shrugs off its characteristic absence of hard fact. 'I am glad I am not to be an archaeologist,' Colquhoun writes at the opening of the chapter called 'Tara of the Kings', 'for my lack of status allows me simply to enjoy myself among antiquities. I can interpret them according to my own morphological intuitions without reference to current ortho-doxies or deference to any school of thought – even without strict regard to evidence.'

(It's worth noting that, despite Colquhoun absolving her-self of the responsibility to interpret detail scientifically, her 1954 stabs at the purpose and function of ancient sites in the Boyne Valley and the Loughcrew Hills, on the slopes of which I proposed to my wife in 2006, were more or less in line with subsequent archaeological opinion.)

While *The Crying of the Wind* responds to Irish history and landscape intuitively, *The Living Stones* is more analytical. And while the Cornish Ithell Colquhoun of *The Living Stones* seems gay and content, her Irish counterpart of three years earlier is fearful of tombs, darkly affected by decaying homesteads and the sufferings of wayfaring tinker children and occasionally vicious towards sections of society she dislikes.

In the chapter entitled 'Roundstone' Colquhoun describes, when drawing outside, how lashings of rain 'spattered on the lines of ink, producing lovely effects that I did not intend'. Where *The Living Stones* is controlled, *The Crying of the Wind* is unmediated, working the elemental and the unpredictable into the writing process.

And while the author of *The Living Stones* is documenting a landscape in which she is happy and where she intends to stay, the Colquhoun of *The Crying of the Wind* seems haunted and restless. And, though I didn't notice it the first time I read the book, upon rereading the chapter 'Night Life' it seems that Colquhoun finds a brief sojourn with bohemian Dublin friends quietly questionable.

During an evening at the famous Gate Theatre she decides that the sainted Oscar Wilde merely 'made the cult of insincerity socially acceptable', before drinking too deeply and too late in the family home of theatrical friends, who stain their absent parents' carpets with red wine and accidentally set fire to the lid of their piano.

In neither of the travel books does Colquhoun offer any obvious clues to her personal history. The character of the narrator of *The Crying of the Wind* arrives from nowhere, without context, experiencing her surroundings in the moment. One paragraph in the chapter 'East to West' leapt out at me as I read the book again, now older and more emotionally vulnerable than when I first enjoyed it as an impregnable younger man.

> The design of the Claddagh wedding-ring, two hands clasping a heart, is famous; but the original rings, heavy and of rough

gold, are scarcely imitated by the flimsy examples displayed in jewellers' shops today. I remember that I nearly chose one of these for my wedding-ring, but the jeweller candidly advised against it, saying it would not wear well. As things happened, it would have proved a more appropriate symbol than the solid gold buckle that I selected instead, which has long outlasted what it betokened.

This odd and uncharacteristically revelatory paragraph is an example of the sort of buried personal detail which, when noticed in tiny shards in Samuel Beckett works such as *Not I*, *Krapp's Last Tape* or the Lucky speech in *Waiting for Godot*, suddenly and irrevocably changes the tone and texture of all the surrounding material by association.

If this peculiar paragraph existed in a book full of personal anecdote it would not seem significant, but it takes on extra weight through the scarcity of comparable revelations. These days all it takes is one swift internet search to substantiate a theoretical subtext.

Colquhoun's five-year marriage to the controversial Russian surrealist Toni del Renzio had ended in divorce six years earlier. In later life her bitterness towards the man she eventually regarded as a 'conman, liar and homosexual' was explicit. Here her sadness and regret seems controlled but very real none the less. (Oddly, one of Toni's roughly contemporaneous lovers, the unfairly neglected Birmingham surrealist Emmy Bridgwater, was eventually to die in 1999 in a newly built house on a new-build estate constructed over the southernmost ellipse of my teenage suburban Solihull paper round.)

It is reasonable to assume Colquhoun's inner landscape was somewhat cloudy and with a chance of heavy rain. Richard Shillitoe, on the website www.ithellcolquhon.co.uk, even suggests that *The Crying of the Wind*, published by her friend Peter Owen was 'an attractive prospect to a small, cost-cutting independent publisher' because the author herself, in this case also an artist, 'was able to supply her own cover artwork and illustrations'.

And, despite the modest success of *The Crying of the Wind*, Owen could not find funding for Colquhoun's proposed Azores-set follow-up, and so the more economically accessed Cornwall was chosen instead. Colquhoun, at this stage, does not appear to be a thoroughly viable prospect.

Was the Colquhoun of the Irish travelogue adrift, professionally, personally? One could read the whole of *The Crying of the Wind* as a kind of pathetic fallacy in reverse as, lost and alone, the blank and blasted author takes on the attributes of the heath itself instead.

The book begins with the writer sleeping, exhausted, in a ruined house and ends, in an apparently perfunctory chapter entitled 'The Municipal Gallery Visited', with her traversing a Dublin art collection looking at portraits, which Colquhoun deems of variable worth, of artists and personages that she decrees of variable value; only Jack Yeats's studies emerge unscathed.

And then it just ends, this mysterious book, with this woman, this mysterious woman, alone in this gallery, the wilds far to the west; the inconclusive conclusion of a story shot through with the kind of endlessly interpretable impressionistic details that Ian Watt and Milan Kundera, in their critical studies *The Rise of the Novel* and *The Art of the Novel* respectively, would identify as examples of peculiarly novelistic knowledge.

The Crying of the Wind may have been intended as a travel book, but its author's curiously unresolved state of mind and the tiny slithers of emotional subtext she lets slip mean it reads like an artfully constructed work of fiction with a carefully calibrated unreliable narrator. *The Crying of the Wind* may be an accidental novel, but it is still a great one.

I moved house two years ago and threshed the chaff from my book collection accordingly. As I transferred *The Crying of the Wind* to the saved stack I noticed something I had never seen before. There was a blue ballpoint-pen inscription, dated July 1961, on the title page: 'To the Parrys, with love from Ithell'. My book was signed by the fucking author, Ithell Fucking Colquhoun, but whichever bookshop had sold it to me hadn't noticed, and neither had I.

'To the Parrys'. The psychologist and publisher John Parry had married Colquhoun's old Slade art-school friend, the surrealist painter and novelist Linda Carmen, in 1940. Carmen sometimes wrote under the name Leo Townsend. Her forgotten artworks were belatedly re-evaluated by John Henshall in the *New Statesman* in 1999.

Linda Carmen died in 1991, three years after Colquhoun herself passed away at the Menwinnion Country House Hotel in her beloved Lamorna. Who had inherited the book Colquhoun gave to Carmen, and how had it found its way to my bookshelf, where this abandoned gift – now one of my favourite works and the edition I own one of my favourite objects – would be treasured?

It's beside me even now, on the bar of the Worcester Travelodge where I write the last few paragraphs of this piece, alone, at 12.34 a.m. on a wet May Monday, drunk on shit wine, after a day of hospital visiting, and I swear this book burns invisibly with its own quiet and consoling heat.

The Ithell Colquhoun of *The Crying of the Wind* would not have allowed herself to impose meaning on this mere coincidence of belated and beloved ownership. The Ithell Colquhoun of *The Living Stones* might have taken some comfort from it. Neither of these prodigiously talented women, I think, would be entirely wrong.

Stewart Lee, writer and clown,
2016

The Liffey Valley

A BUMPY AVENUE seemed to lead through parkland – a favourite Irish technique in road repair is to fill the pot-holes with pebbles and leave the traffic to level them. Then there was the stone-flagged hall of a Georgian house and a clamour of voices. Someone suggested a bath and sleep for me, and I gladly acquiesced.

A long, narrow bedroom housed a bath and lavatory, and ancient family photographs by Eliot and Fry – the figures posed as conversation pieces – shared the walls with John Leach's sporting prints. There must have been a vogue once for the latter as bathroom décor, for I remember them at my grandparents' house. The water was surprisingly hot.

My room was large and dim; it was uncarpeted and not very quiet, since it backed on to the plumbing of the bathroom. But I slept at first from sheer exhaustion.

The household consisted of five ageing sisters – perhaps only Ireland could produce such a ménage. Four were unmarried; the remaining one, a widow, had her younger son with her. The father used to live in great style, keeping up a huge country place and entertaining lavishly; but he was ashamed to admit, if approached by a suitor, that he could provide each daughter with only a hundred pounds a year. He would accordingly dismiss with abuse any eligible swain, and so tyrannized over the girls that they trembled even to meet him on the staircase, meanwhile continuing to live far beyond his means. Only the youngest daughter married, and that was after his death when the place had to be sold. Still holding to a traditional way of life which they had not the money to support, they pooled their resources and courageously maintained a semblance of it by running a guest-house.

The sisters all talked loudly and at once, no one listening, each of them intent on expressing her own reactions. Except the eldest, who was a semi-invalid, all worked hard in house and garden but without any organization and so with some waste of effort. There was much bickering, but the animal unity of the clan remained unbroken beneath superficial scratches.

Their setting was almost Spanish in its mingled nobility and shabbiness. The plasterwork of the ceilings, the ironwork of the fireplaces were fine, and the flowers grown in the garden were set in Crown Derby vases. The wallpaper in the drawing-room, an exquisite pale-gold pattern on white, was more than a hundred years old – they all mounted ladders when they first moved into the house and cleaned the whole of it with bread. But the huge rooms had little heating; windows and doors did not fit, letting in all too easily the damp and chill of the Irish climate. What matter if carpets were seldom swept, for the food was good, much of it produced in the garden and farmstead.

A park and woodland at the back of the house sloped to the Liffey, and in the evening I went there with J. to collect firewood. There was no turf to burn in the neighbouring countryside, and other fuels were expensive. Under towering trees the white of garlic in flower gave the illusion of a snowfall, and its sickly smell made me feel faint. Beside a ramshackle fishing hut flowed the river; dark, suddenly rippled, 'she ninnygoes, nannygoes, nancing by'. Upstream was a mill by a weir, salmon rising in the quieter reaches. Thunder was in the air but no rain. J. made a bundle of the fallen branches we had found and carried it home in an old tweed coat.

I spent the next morning at work in the studio, a spacious room with three long windows, almost unfurnished and completely unheated. In a household of this kind there are always dogs to be exercised, and later on I took them for a walk. (A breeder in the neighbourhood was said to have 'nests of dogs'.) Clouds had been heavy all day, and now rain was beginning to fall, pitting the Liffey's tranquil glide. Belated primroses lurked in the sopping grass, and above them thorn blossom burdened the hedges.

There was white asphodel in the luxuriant herbaceous border of the south garden and red broom like raw flesh. How do subtropical plants survive in this climate, much colder than anything in the south of England? Beneath one of the enormous yews of the walled garden grew a plant of drooping form, like those of the lily-of-the-valley tribe, but its waxen flowers were composite. Untrimmed thorn hedges, also grown to immense size like the yews, supported a tangle of ivy and wild clematis that scrambled to their highest twigs and cascaded down again almost hiding the walls, which were castellated in places and topped with rank valerian. There I found the Davidia, a Chinese tree taller than the yews and covered with flowers like handkerchiefs or small flags attached to it by one corner. It reminded me of the fig tree of St Salomoné near Paphos, where devotees tear a strip from their clothing to hang upon the branches above the sacred well. I have heard that this custom, still usual in the Middle East, lingers also in Ireland, and the association of tree, well and votive tatters may be found here, too, though the fig or olive is replaced by an isolated thorn.

There are skies in Ireland as nowhere else; clouds that seem full of ink, the clear spaces beyond them appallingly metallic; masses of vapour stretching themselves for miles, half detached from the cloud's main body; or an impermeable weight, heavy as a castle with an edge of 'terrible crystal'. There is always an alienating contrast, as the misty and the dazzling, the massive and the slight, the dense and the transparent. This character of the heavens is due, I suppose, to an intense clearness, coming from the comparative absence of industrial pollution, and to the great humidity, so that the atmosphere, already free of the worst grimes, is yet continually washed in a medium that veils any strident glare. There is only one thing better than a fine day in England and that is a fine day in Ireland – and not only because of its rarity. Perhaps a fine day in Kerry is best of all, when the air is like a diamond yet the dews are never far away.

A pair of hawks, in size between kestrel and buzzard, with the buzzard's spiral flight – what were they? Enviable birds, lifted above the enclosing earth. The valley of the Liffey is somewhat oppressive here, rather like a vaster and greener Weybridge. Neither district is true country but land parcelled out as residential plots, one garden (or in this case, one park) bordering the next with no space between and, as far as the eye can see, no space beyond – an all-too-'settled ground'. It even reminds one of *Huis Clos*:

> GARCIN: Et au bout de ce couloir?
> LE GARÇON: Il y a d'autres chambres et d'autres couloirs.

But this, after all, is only the Ireland of the Pale; beyond it, somewhere, is wildness.

Many families lead the traditional life of gentry in spite of straitened means. Levelling influences have taken longer to become apparent, the cost of living is somewhat lower, servants slightly easier to come by and (often the deciding factor) standards of comfort less exacting. Big houses are lived in here long after they have ceased to be, by English standards, in habitable repair and lacking, as they often do, the most elementary conveniences. 'The county' doesn't mind shabbiness or even squalor so long as your politics, your religion and your accent are 'right'.

J. told us a story of how he was once trying to buy a

greyhound from a woman who bred them in one of these dilapidated country places. When he entered the vast central hall, where swarms of bats were flittering among the rafters and rain dripping in through numerous leaks, he found his hostess lying in a drunken stupor beside the embers of a turf fire. When at last he was able to rouse her, she led him unsteadily to the back premises where the hounds were kept. The litter from which he was to select the puppy had not yet been born, but if the promised greyhound was not evident, the greyhounds' larder certainly was, for hunks of horseflesh and half-flayed bullocks' heads hung from the surrounding trees. J. was not sorry to take leave of this macabre establishment, where, needless to say, his deal was never satisfactorily completed.

In another house I heard of, rats were treated as domestic pets. They were allowed to spring upon a dresser, breaking its store of priceless china, and to chew the hem of the eighteenth-century curtains, embroidered in scarlet and white beads, which hung in the many tall windows. These were examples of the big house in decline, approached, though seldom equalled by, many another domain in Ireland, which, once the centre of an almost self-supporting community and the focus of a variety of skills, has been left all but deserted. Heavy drinking, though, is less characteristic of the Anglo-Irish than of some of their neighbours, and indeed they often make their first economies on alcohol.

Though politically almost unrepresented and economically all but insolvent, the Protestant Ascendency is still, strange to say, in the ascendant socially. The BBC is popular, and Radio Éireann is seldom switched on except for racing results; to speak with a brogue is to be frowned upon, and one goes to church on Ascension Day to offset the mass-going Catholics. All this, together with a rather shocking snobbery, is a defence mechanism to keep intact a dwindling community and to demonstrate it as a race apart. There is a feeling of 'us folk' (the

Protestant Anglo-Irish) as distinct from 'they' (the Catholic Celtic Irish); in describing it one can hardly help slipping into a Kiplingesque jargon. One would scarcely be surprised to hear the Catholic Irish referred to as natives! And this in 1954; yet, up to now, these tactics have had some success, though how long they can continue to stave off the inevitable dissolution it is difficult to say.

Perhaps the most effective link between members of this group is the Church of Ireland, which draws its no mean vitality from social and political loyalties rather than religious fervour. Though English life is still the standard, it is the life of last century, and today it is easy enough to distinguish the English from the Anglo-Irish visitors at a country hotel on a Sunday morning. The English lounge about, but the Anglo-Irish go to the Church of Ireland (kept firmly locked at all other times) less, perhaps, for devotional purposes than to hear the news, see their friends and generally keep in touch. If the hotel proprietors are Protestants there is a little ceremony afterwards at midday with coffee served to the church-goers, presumably as a reward for their demonstration of solidarity. No doubt it is the power of these totems and taboos that gives some Anglo-Irish households, in spite of their slovenliness, an atmosphere of constriction. They are not really devil-may-care, happy-go-lucky or any of the things that Irish households are supposed (in England) to be.

The family in the Lucan valley patronized the local church, except J. and his mother, who went to a special church in Dublin, the Irish equivalent of High Anglican. Most Protestant churches are as low as it is possible to be: incense is the reek of the 'scarlet woman', coloured vestments are despised and even the altar cross is sometimes banished as a Romish bauble. The reverse process may be observed elsewhere, for the Church of Scotland tends to be high to distinguish itself from the Presbyterians. What animal is the chameleon's opposite, taking on, instead of protective colouring, the hue complementary to that of its nearest neighbour?

It is difficult in Ireland to be a cosy old agnostic, for if you are not a Catholic you get classed as a Protestant. However, I managed to escape into the woods where the Liffey, overhung by enormous trees, had been stirred up by recent rains and showed pale opaque brown instead of dark topaz and was spotted with foam. I paddled in the shallows, though the wind, blowing out of an almost cloudless sky, had an edge to it as always in Ireland.

Slender-legged colts stepped down the opposite bank to drink; they pawed the water nervously, seeming to want it muddy before tasting it. Perhaps they were not thoroughbreds, but they had a wild grace now seldom seen in English fields. None the less, I was thankful that the wide expanse of the current divided me from them, for I regard any horse as a psychotic with homicidal tendencies and prefer to avoid close quarters. It is not so long since I cowered in a craggy cleft by the shore on one of the Scilly Islands while colts and fillies, gay with spring fever, chased one another up and down a miniature Camargue.

In the decaying shanty or disused fishing-hut structure – which I had read about in *The Mysteries of Udolpho* but had never before seen – was hidden the nest of a wren. I watched the little creature flying in and out of the globe it had constructed by matting together dead leaves.

Dublin

As OFTEN HERE, rain overtook a fine morning at midday; in Fitzwilliam Square the air, almost warm, was burdened with the scent of laburnum, red may, pink may, lilac. This is a city with little feeling of claustrophobia, for the Dublin Mountains are always visible beyond; and from this square they seem, in some lights, tantalizingly near. Low clouds part, and the clearness of the air suddenly reveals them, strong purple, then a shadow, a veil of rain sweeps across, and nothing is left of them but mist. A few minutes later the veil thins and they appear beyond it, obscurely blue; or a sudden shaft of sunlight tears it open, and the lower slopes come forward in their native green, their bracken-grown sides seeming, at this distance, like banks of moss. They change colour and texture with all the weather's freaks.

These hills have no great height nor, like the Sugar Loaf Mountains to the south in Wicklow, spectacular outline. But they have a luring look, and it was to them that 'Æ' as a poor boy, only just able to afford the tram fare to the outskirts of town, would escape from the 'boredom of the desk'. It was while wandering over their flanks and folds that he saw his first visions of the Earth Spirit and discovered his 'fountains out of Hecate'.

Though the racket of mechanical transport has long invaded the Dublin streets, its noise is less devastating than in London. Crowding in, closing in, stupefication from deafening – all are mitigated here.

In St Stephen's Green, which since *Ulysses* has seemed

to be named for Stephen Dedalus, I saw one of Anna Livia Plurabelle's many daughters skurrying along beside the Shelbourne Hotel. Or was it Anna Livia herself? Joyce describes her light-heartedly, seeing in her the comic aspect of the Cailleách, that ageless ambiguous multiparous figure that haunts the hinterland of folklore in all Celtic countries:

> as soon as they saw her meander by that maritime way in her grasswinter's weeds and twigged whom she was under her deaconess bonnet . . . Everyone that saw her said that the dowce little delia looked a bit queer . . . Kickhams a frumpier ever you saw.

But to me she appeared in tragic guise, teeny, ageing and twisted, with burning eyes in parchment skin, a rusty-black kerchief tied over her head, coat ragged, stockings in shreds. She was so fragile that 'a fourpenny bit in each pocketside weighed her safe from the blowaway windrush'. Seeing her, one sees the result of the Church's indifference to well-being, knowledge, power as compared to that thin flame, often unrecognized by the human candle which it consumes, which is the one thing necessary.

The contrast between this pathetic whisp – burned away, blown along, who knows whither? – and the sleek, full-fed types lounging with their feet up along the Shelbourne's terrace was striking and now almost forgotten in England, where one hardly remembers the sight of really poor people. But here tattered clothes, collar held together by a bent safety-pin, teeth untended in the absence of a health service – one need not look far to find them. Sometimes in the slummier quarters, in the Dublin of the exquisite doorway and broken fanlight, one finds, as in Italian streets, a golden-brown child with the skin, the eyes and the curls of a quattrocento *angelin*, a type unbred by the welfare state.

Nor is the beauty of Irish skins a legend only; one sees many that owe nothing of their smoothness to cosmetics or of their clear colour to exterior aids. Some are of that frail type which freckles easily; others, more durable, keep their white and carmine in any weather. And it is not only complexions that compare well with England; good looks in general, both in women and men, are more frequent here. Thick hair, clear eyes fringed with those famous lashes that mascara can never imitate, fine features, well-proportioned bodies and a good carriage – what is the cause? Race, climate, food, absence of industrialization? Who knows! Sometimes it is no more than good health and the well-being this gives, but sometimes there is also an unusual delicacy of feature and sweetness of expression. In the women there is perhaps a lingering knowledge that beauty is different from smartness, that it cannot be taken from dressing-table and wardrobe and applied to oneself – however much outward grooming may help to 'present' it, give it stage presence.

Tall houses along Aston's Quay are painted scarlet and other bright colours, one more reminder that a channel divides one from England. But the last of the bookstalls along the quays, that used to remind one of Paris, disappeared before the war; cinema and radio make for illiteracy, and in a country of small population their results are obvious. I could find only one second-hand bookshop in this quarter where once were several; I wanted to look inside it but tried in vain to enter, for it seemed to have been locked for months. There were some interesting works in the window, all coated with undisturbed dust.

In the bus returning along the Lucan Road I recognized the 'Fiendish Park' by the immense phallic column of the Wellington Obelisk and glimpsed 'the dove of the dunas' in Chapelizod with its garage dedicated to Isolda.

Glendalough

J .'s VAN PROVIDED a bumpy lift into Dublin; so rough was it that I advised against using it for our trip into Connemara.

I should have missed my bus for Glendalough if it had not been ten minutes late in starting. I was told that had it been full before it might well have left ten minutes early instead! Time has a different value here; even in a city the anxious pressure of it is slackened, and the well-known anecdote about the two clocks at the railway station is not exaggerated.

The coast road passed through Dún Laoghaire; Dalkey of the seven castles that crowns its burlesque king every year on a smooth green island just off the coast; Killiney, with its Druids' Chair rocks hiding among well-spaced villas on the hillside above the sheltered strand; Bray, dwarfed by the two Sugar Loaf Mountains, outposts of the main Wicklow range. Rows of neat modern houses are everywhere encroaching on the untamed land; England's tyranny has been thrown off, but the smugness of English suburban life has seeped subtly back into the new Ireland. Comfort, hygiene and respectability are apparent along this eastern coast; the picturesque beggary that still lurks in the cities, and also in the wilder parts, is absent here.

The Rocky Road crosses the Dargle and leaves the wide demesne of Powerscourt on the right below, then carries on to Roundwood and the tamed lakes of the Vartry reservoir, Annamoe, Laragh, where several glens meet, and at last Glendalough.

When I first caught sight of the mountain above the lower

lake I held my breath and stared – spellbound not so much by its loveliness as because I recognized it from a dream. Long ago, before I first went to Ireland, I dreamed of a cone-shaped mountain, pinkish in colour, with sparse conifers growing up the sides. I made a drawing of it, thinking it must be Mount Errigal, which I should soon be seeing. But when its immense pale pyramid, bare of vegetation, rose before me from the Donegal uplands, I knew I was wrong. And I found embodied at Glendalough the mountain of my dream, the same conical slope made pinkish by its covering of dead bracken, a background for scattered fir trees.

Two objects here, relics of stone-worship, are said to bring good luck if the right ritual is observed. You embrace the shaft of the tall sixth-century cross of St Kevin, its head sculptured with biblical scenes, and make your wish meanwhile; it is obvious what kind of wish such observances were originally deemed likely to grant. A few steps further on you cross the Avonmore, still very small, and come upon a group of much older stones. On one of these you must sit without support for the feet and, leaning over to your right, dip a hand in the water of the basin-shaped Deer Stone. St Kevin – Christianized avatar of the local genius here, as Kieran is at Clonmacnoise, Buithe at Monasterboice and Finbarr at Gougane-barra – adopted an infant whose mother had died in giving it birth. Having nothing with which to feed it, he induced a wild deer to allow herself to be milked each day into this rocky basin and so provide nourishment for the child.

Deer in Irish legend are often semi-human; as part of the widespread magical tradition of shape-shifting, they take on human form or offer their bodies as temporary disguise for human beings. When St Patrick set out to convert the hosts of the hostile King Laoghaire on Tara's hill, he and his monks were changed seemingly into wild deer, and to this day the hymn, or rather incantation, which he then sang is called 'The

Deer's Cry'. This title well fits the pre-Christian elements to be found in it, such as the pantheistic invocation of the elements:

> I arise today
> Through the strength of heaven:
> Light of sun
> Radiance of moon
> Splendour of fire
> Speed of lightning
> Swiftness of wind
> Depth of sea
> Stability of earth,
> Firmness of rock

or the phrase where he asks protection 'Against spells of women and smiths and wizards'. The other name of the poem, 'St Patrick's Breastplate', suggests its later additions and adaptations.

Like Clonmacnoise, Cong and Monasterboice, Glendalough was one of the chief centres of learning in the Ireland of the Dark Ages; there are said to be the ruins of seven churches here, four of which I located. Holy Trinity, little more than foundations, lay beside the road approaching the lower lake; nearer the water was the roofless cathedral; the Oratory, called St Kevin's Kitchen, once had a croft roof and was since used to house an old stone cross, an inscribed slab and other ancient stone remains; and the tiny Teampull na Skellig could only be reached by taking a boat across the upper lake to where it stood under a mountainous slope of the southern shore. Hollowed in the rocky face above was St Kevin's Bed, a cave just large enough to lie in. Pursued by his sweetheart Kathleen even to this austere couch, the saint pushed her into the water rather than risk seduction. (Murder, it seems, was less serious.) But another version of the story, less ungallant though no less pious, says that she slipped from his precarious eyrie into the lake, whereupon Kevin instantly plunged to her rescue. The ducking cooled her ardour, and she subsequently became a nun.

Many visitors – with the notable exception of Thackeray, who found the atmosphere of the place innocent and friendly – have felt Glendalough to be gloomy and sinister. There are stories of hauntings around the upper lake; it is one of the many 'bottomless' lakes of Ireland, always associated in the popular mind with an entrance to the Underworld, like the classical Avernus. Here the water certainly seemed blacker than that of the lower lake, perhaps because surrounded almost completely by steep mountainsides; but its surface was scarcely disturbed by a frisson of the uncanny. To be sure, it was a bright day; in bad weather it must seem grim enough.

The late Art O'Murnaghan once told me that he had seen, while on the slopes above the upper lake, large phantasmal forms drifting down into the water in broad daylight. He described them as resembling airborne tarpaulins, not cloudy or indistinct but quite palpable. I do not disbelieve him; what he saw appears to belong to a definite, if little-understood, class of rural haunting. Such entities are not ghosts in the ordinary sense; they are neither brute nor human nor ever have been, though perhaps one could call them the animals of some preternatural world. They belong to the countryside; they have their favourite habitat like any wild creature; and like other outdoor things they can easily be missed by those who do not know what to look for. Some will sense their terrain by a half-formed feeling of eeriness, though nothing may be seen, and particular conjunctions of light and atmospheric density will help to make them visible.

Their forms vary; a friend described one she had seen on some downs in Dorsetshire as being 'the size of a haystack, opaque but fluid at the edges, moving very quickly'; another is sometimes seen like a tower racing over wide sands on the north coast of Cornwall. I have myself seen in Cornwall one like a massive pillar of unknown substance, with filaments stretched from the top seemingly to hold it to the ground like the guy-ropes of a tent.

Those who think such beings inimical to human life are right, in that many wild creatures distrust (with reason) man's approach. But that they would molest humanity if not first molested, I do not believe. Our life is to them alien and disturbing, and they will protect themselves from it if need be, but their natural attitude is unconcern rather than hostility. They follow their own unthinkable life, mobile to some extent, yet rooted by impalpable threads to some piece of earth as yet uncontaminated by urban enclosure, without mind, without emotion, without purpose as we know it. Who can assess their place in the scheme of things – are they relics of some earlier world? They exist; that is all we can say. We share the cosmos with them.

Some perhaps have been partially tamed as village gods, may even have assumed a half-human form in response to the desire of those cultivating them, for their tenuous substance reacts, it is said, to a powerful image projected upon it. Others again, less domesticated, are those creatures which Lamaism calls Yidags or Horrid Beings and classified into thirty-six species under such names as Eaters of Mist, Scarcely Seen, Earth Lurkers. Those who call them elementals are misleading, for they are a different tribe from the spirits of the four elements in the Paracelsian system.

The graveyard of Glendalough, once that of the monastic community, is still in use, for I saw a girl with long red hair tending a grave. Her dress was of pale raspberry colour, the coat a darker shade, making with her hair an unpremeditated harmony. Five crosses once formed the march of the community's land; I only discovered one, much mutilated, standing in the grass at the roadside below the upper lake, where a new car-park was being made. One can only hope that the others have not fallen victim to the bulldozer as have too many antiquities, to say nothing of natural beauties, during and since the war.

When we passed through the small town of Rathdrum, flags were stretched across the streets in honour of the Marian Year, centenary of the proclaiming as a dogma of the Immaculate Conception. We overtook a funeral with but few flowers decking the bier and followed only by men on foot, as is the custom.

In Ireland people still know how to relax, though with less of the grace and animal passivity of Arabs on the quay of a North African port. But one sees them lounging on the grassy verge of the road – here a buxom girl in purple satin lying at full length, hands clasped behind her head.

We followed a tree-tunnelled road through strangely flower-less woods – in Lamorna they would be full of bluebells and campion at this season – to the Vale of Avoca and the Meeting of the Waters of the rivers Avonmore and Avonbeg. Here was the tree, now a mere skeleton railed in, reclining beneath which Tom Moore is supposed to have written his poem on this place. A plaque repeated a quatrain from it, in the prancing dactylic measure of which he was fond, and a bust of him surmounted yet another wishing-stone with its small pool of water. I dipped in my hand with the same wish as ever; it never varies, for well or shooting star or the first strawberry.

Much as I should like to praise every manifestation of the Celtic fire, I cannot feel that Moore was a great poet or more than a fluent versifier. Like many another, he had the poetic temperament without the maker's capacity; he saw intensely, he felt keenly, he gave himself time to brood – and he produced nothing but jingles. He lacked the revealer's insight and so any mantic command of language; he was master of none but the shallowest tinkle of music. Alas, much the same must be said of Griffin and Mangan, though Mangan achieved more in 'Siberia' than in his famous 'Dark Rosaleen'. Both Walsh and Callanan gave echoes of something grander, especially Callanan when he translated from the Irish.

In the road above the rivers twisting their two strands, an outside-car was standing, now almost a relic of the past. One no longer sees them in Dublin or any of the larger towns, where all is mechanized, but a few remain in Killarney and other tourist centres as survivals of the picturesque still able to earn a little. The driver was wearing the remains of traditional dress, with a handkerchief knotted around his neck and high-crowned hat of hairy felt. His pale face reflected the pathos of a fast-vanishing epoch; he seemed resigned to neglect, for not even visitors were employing him, preferring their own smart automobiles, and he was too fatalistic even to solicit custom from them. He was thin, and when he got down from his car I saw that he was lame also; perhaps plying his outside-car for hire was all he could do for a living. The new Ireland was passing him by; victim of time, he was yet untouched by it – fey, quiet, weather-worn, wiry, he recalled a certain type of Kerryman whom one meets on the bog roads with his cart of turf or watches putting out to sea in his curragh from a tiny green-water bay. One sees him, too, in the pictures of Jack Yeats (surely one of the greatest artists in the painterly tradition now living) standing on some desolate jetty and gazing entranced at the misty water beyond or leaning across a bar – figures not single yet each wrapped in his own ambience which also is, or was, the life of the community, the holy unconscious.

I remember particularly one painting which I saw in Jack Yeats's studio some years ago; it depicted three or four elderly men wading breast-high into a cold-looking sea at twilight. Country people do not care for sea bathing as a rule, but on some evening at summer's end, say in September or October, the older men would wade out to sea for what must once have been a ceremonial lustration or a propitiation of that very old man of the sea, King Lir.

How different was this sad and isolated jarvey of the Meeting of the Waters from those of Killarney, famous for their tall stories and extravagant jokes! On our commenting upon the bad weather to one of these, he told us that it had once rained for nine years without stopping! 'But that', he added as a concession to plausibility, 'was in India.'

The Vale of Avoca was open, pretty country but not spectacular in any way and, after the praises heaped upon it, disappointing. Southward, the shafts and engine houses of disused mines jutted from the hillsides; but, as in so many places in Cornwall, their hint of industrialization no longer jarred, having become acclimatized, weathered, partially overgrown. Further down the valley towards Woodenbridge, however, some mines had lately been reopened for sulphur and ochre, and pyramids of vivid gravel, though fascinating in their way, disturbed the sylvan scene.

The valley had very steep sides above Clara, 'smallest village in Ireland', which consisted of a church, a school and the schoolmaster's house. He and his family were the only inhabitants, a population of five. Halfway up the cliff above, a white figure showed up clearly against a screen, the shrine of Our Lady of Clara. Others like her, white or white and blue, had been set up at several places in the neighbourhood. In each case, perhaps, some local portent had chosen their site, though it usually recalled that of Bernadette's vision of 'the Lady' – a rocky cleft surrounded by undergrowth. These shrines, and the crosses erected at high points among the Wicklow Mountains, attempt to dominate the unsanctified heart of nature, which must remain for ever unredeemed.

Though claimed by the Catholic Church, the Apparition of Lourdes did not manifest herself to one religious group only, nor did she herself ever claim to be the Blessed Virgin. When

Bernadette asked her who she was she hesitated a long time before replying, and finally declared, 'I am the Immaculate Conception.' She thus stressed her kinship with the world of impersonal ideas rather than with that of personified deities.

What did she really look like, this figure who has inspired so much of the sugary artifice in present-day ecclesiastical sculpture and *oggetti religiosi*? These certainly do not reflect what Bernadette saw. When shown religious pictures from various schools of painting, she rejected the insipid modern representations, picking out a Siennese Madonna as the closest approximation to her vision. This shows her good taste at least, even if it proves nothing about the value of her story.

Forced to recognize the preternatural by a countryside in close contact with it, man shies away from the utterly other, clothing in human form his intuition of hidden powers.

Lucan

O N A BRIGHT windy morning I walked to Lucan, which, though hardly more than a village, has been a tiny spa since the eighteenth century, with one huge hotel overlooking the river. The valley of the Liffey opens out here, the southern bank growing less steep; opposite, mills have been built above a weir. The wooded setting would be delightful but for the devastating noise of traffic on the main road from Dublin to the west, Galway and Sligo, which passes through it.

Even in the Sarsfield demesne one cannot escape its vibration, for the road runs alongside. The turnstile, set in a building that seemed like a disused coach house, was unattended, so I walked in without a ticket. The pathway plunged immediately into close shrubberies, tunnelling on viewlessly for some distance, then widened a little as it gave upon the Grotto House, cold in the woodland shade. The arched interior had a certain Mediterranean charm, but the blue wash on the walls of the Oratory was scrawled with signatures, somehow obscene in effect, though no coarse words could be deciphered. The holy well beside it was stagnant and stuffed with branches – a deliberate desecration, for they could not have fallen there by chance.

This defiling of a well, as I found when I reached the west, is a recognized method of showing one's dislike; the water is spoiled with grass, leaves or sticks; or, if the owner is very unpopular, a dead cat is thrown in. Though a symbolic as well as a utilitarian expression of hostility, it may, as a material frustration, be serious enough on a small island, where drinking-water is scarce and wells perhaps fill only spasmodically. Perhaps it originated in the belief that the first water drawn from a well on May Day was an antidote to evil spells; the first person to reach it after midnight would throw in grass to show that the purity had already been taken.

I could not help contrasting this abused shrine with the magical peace of Madron Baptistery in Penwith, hidden by a silvery thicket of sallows far from the road. There the ruined chapel is open to the sky, but the walls have recently been built up and are now cared for, though mosses and ferns are not banished from their crannies. The water pours through a grotto at one corner of the enclosure, overflowing its basin and gushing freely across the shaven grass of the floor and out to the sloping copseland beyond. Still more hidden, though only a few yards away, an older well lifts a placid surface to catch light filtered to it through tufts of herbage. The quiet of the atmosphere is not broken but only made more serene by small birds' tinkling cries. It is the scene of individual rites only as of coin or pin; but the baptistery is used in both Church and Chapel ceremonies during the first days of May. It is beyond denominations, like the well in the garden of Matariyah near Cairo, venerated by pagans, Moslems and Christians alike.

The demesne path led up and down, still without a view, traversing impacted evergreens. An immense conifer of seven stems, its roots heaving to link with one another above ground like those of a banyan, rose upwards on my left. A feeling of sadistic menace hung over the place, and this was not dispersed when I left the confines of the wood some distance further on and began to cross an open parkland. Rather did it increase as I approached the end of the demesne and Sarsfield's Cottage, a small building in rustic style, now reaching the last stages of dilapidation. There was no sign of the 'Refreshments' said to be obtainable, the last whiskey and sausage roll must long ago have been consumed. Below and to the right the river spread out, haunted by an ill-tempered swan; two frail wooden structures, intended as changing-rooms, were falling into disrepair. There were no bathers. A fragile landing-stage projected a little over the water, but not a boat was to be seen.

What can have happened here? It was all I could do to walk up to the cottage, the miasma of horror about the place was so strong, stimulating phantasies of sexual attack. How came this air of corruption to be connected with Patrick Sarsfield, Earl of Lucan, the heroic defender of Limerick, whose final capitulation, with honourable terms dishonourably violated, started the Flight of the Wild Geese?

Still followed by a sense of menace, I retraced my steps, no other way back seeming possible, to the deserted coach house at the entry. I then took another path through the bushes, this time leading to Sarsfield's Castle, the patriot's birthplace. Soon a three-storey keep hung with appalling ivy of a breed unusually long-leaved, and with the massive lianas of wild clematis, stood before me. I entered the dusk of the ground-floor room which had once served as a chapel and opened upon a constricted graveyard full of broken crosses and headstones. I glanced at these melancholy relics but made no attempt to climb to the upper storeys, though a narrow doorway promised an upwards-winding stair.

Once more outside, I gazed up at the tumbling creepers and wondered, as often before, at Ireland's vegetation – how does it attain this subtropical luxuriance, support these exotic species? Surely the climate cannot account for it – the wind is always cold, even on a fine day, and one scarcely ever needs summer clothes, except perhaps occasionally in some sheltered bay of the south. Rain is almost continuous, and snow is frequent, sending icy gusts over the flatter country from whitened peaks throughout the long winter. I shall never forget landing once at Shannon Airport in the last days of March and seeing what appeared to be huge pyramids of salt on the horizon. They were, in fact, the Galtee Mountains, and I could scarcely believe that their covering from base to summit was snow, for the weather in London, though far from spring-like, had not prepared me for such rigours. The wind soon confirmed the visual impression; and as late as the first week in May I saw the whole of that range of the Dingle Peninsula, which culminates in Mount Brandon, inches deep in snow. Yet fuchsias survive in the most exposed places, and I have seen arum lilies growing wild on the Kerry coast in the teeth of the bitterest gales. Numbers of introduced plants thrive miraculously in gardens.

As I returned over the green at the edge of Lucan, boys were playing hurling, most popular of the traditional games. I lay sunbathing all the afternoon, the woods sheltering me from the keenest of the wind. Later, as I wandered down a lane, I came upon a gatepost shaped like a miniature round-tower, even the conical cap being imitated in metal. I made a drawing of it, determining to compare it with the example at Clondalkin a few miles distant.

Accordingly I persuaded one of the sisters to drive me there in the late evening. We set out in her minute ramshackle car, she resolutely taking the wrong side of the road. (In Ireland there is no test for motorists – if you know how to start a car, you can simply buy one and drive it away.) I am not a nervous passenger, not being a driver myself, but I must confess that my heart missed a beat whenever a heavy truck approached. However, we arrived without making any addition to her record of accidents.

Clondalkin, like Palmerston, is one of the villages in Dublin's neighbourhood which during the last ten years have succumbed to suburban development, losing their identity to the speculative builder and other commercial interests. My gatepost, in fact, had the more romantic setting, for Clondalkin's tower, perfect as it is, has now been out-topped by factory chimneys, and advancing industrialization has choked the surrounding fields. But both gatepost and tower must derive from some archetype in the morphology of the country's genius, neither imitating the other, but springing from a common source which is now, alas, being more completely obliterated year by year.

East to West

A MORNING OF foggy dew enveloped the start of our drive across the central plain, from Liffey Valley to Connemara coast. I was thankful that the idea of going in J.'s van had been abandoned at the last moment, and we decided instead to hire a car and take J. along as driver.

To a passenger in a car, the noise of the main road through Lucan was less shattering than to a pedestrian. There is a good surface for motoring, and, once the branch to Mullingar that takes one ultimately to Sligo is passed and one heads due west, the volume of traffic is halved. As one goes on, the road becomes emptier still and pleasanter for driving than any road of comparable importance in England.

At Leixlip we crossed the Royal Canal connecting Dublin with Mullingar and soon passed Maynooth, the grim structures of its seminary exuding, as often with this type of institution, an aura of unacknowledged evil, cold and oppressive. Then Kilcock, a market town with a single wide, untidy street – an example of that gulf in Ireland's architecture between thatched cabin and Georgian mansion, filled with slate and galvanized iron and concrete unimaginatively used. But sometimes the dullness of a small provincial town is relieved by *trompe-l'œil* tiles, usually in black and white, painted on the rendered façade of a shop or dwelling. These dazzle-patterns are amusing, and from the nineteenth century there still remain a number of shop-fronts with decorative lettering based on the 'Egyptian' typefaces of the Victorian era, though these are gradually giving way to the milk-bar type of vulgarity. A few places like Kilkenny survive, however, with their shopfronts almost intact, and many charming examples lingered, until a few years ago at least, in Killorglin of Puck Fair fame.

But townscape can take little part in any drive through Ireland, for most of the country is still rural. All along our route I was able to pick out prehistoric sites – ráth, dún, liss, artificial mounds and enclosures of all kinds – apart from the more obvious ruined church, neglected graveyard or dismantled keep. This is not difficult, once you know what to look for, even from a car or a train. Before coming into Kinnegad we crossed the Boyne Valley, whose whole length is stored with antiquities. A signpost on the left pointed to Edenderry, a neighbourhood that would have yielded much, I feel sure, could I have explored it. The Oaks of Eden! The sound of the name suggested the morning of Gaeldom, priestly circumambulations beneath patriarchal trees, shafts of early sunlight glinting on robe and knife. But my phantasy depended on a pun, for the literal translation of the Irish name is simply Oakwood Hill-Brow.

On either side of the road a country of flat pasture stretched away to exploration's bound, sketchily divided by thorn hedges gone wild, their blossom muted today by the misty air. The fields were occasionally cut by an avenue leading to a 'place' and became more park-like; less often, a russet patch of bogland intervened, but this was rare, for most of the great Bog of Allen, which once covered the whole central plain, is now reclaimed for grassland. Towards Tyrrellspass the country grew more undulating; this land belonged to an Anglo-Norman family, themselves earlier dispossessors, until they were dispossessed by Cromwell.

Some localities have an 'airy' (eerie) quality perceptible even through the insulation of a mechanical conveyance, and these are not always the sites of greatest archaeological interest. Such are the eskers, whose appeal is rather to the geologist – immense moraines, relict of glacial epochs but long since covered with green, that heave across Ireland as rampart-like hills, intersecting it from east to west, their sides as smooth as if constructed by the hand of man. I caught a glimpse of one near Kilbeggan and another at Moate, though the name here is taken not from the esker but from the artificial mound of Gráinne Óg.

At last we left Leinster and entered Connacht by the bridge spanning a wide reach of the Shannon at Athlone. An ancient stronghold, King John's castle, stood beside it, and near at hand was the cathedral, said to be built to a plan of St Peter's at Rome in miniature. It was market day, but the squealing of pigs that floated in through the open doorway in nowise disturbed the people who knelt with entranced gaze towards the high altar.

Few of them could know that they were above the Ford of the Loin, the loin of the white-horned Finnbenach, Connacht's Bull, who was also the west and the onset of night, for was he not 'cornutus' like the moon? He underwent an Osirian dismemberment at the horns of his rival, Ulster's Brown Bull of Cooley, whose back was broad enough for the play of fifty children and who, when angry, would stamp his keeper thirty feet into the ground. He tossed the White Horned after their battle on the Plain of Aei, scattering his fragment to the winds of Ireland, and here fell his loin. Swineherds once to the race of divinities, these rivals had become in turn ravens, sea monsters, warriors, demons and finally bulls, though not mere creatures of the herd but aspects of the sky and the year.

We bought food for lunch, and, driving out beyond the confines of the town, we turned along a lane to look for a place to picnic. The sun had penetrated its veil of mist and shed a faint silvery warmth over the daisied grass. We stopped at a field where ducks were wading in a stream and in the shelter of a low wall ate our slices of ham, eggs, salad and the favourite barm brack or currant loaf (*breac* meaning speckled) and drank cider.

After Athlone the landscape roughened in character, and the fields, grown smaller, were marked off by stone walls instead of straggling hedges, for with Ballinasloe the country of the Galway Blazers was approaching. After Athenry, the King's Ford, the first mountains of Connacht began to show pale in the west, and then, quite suddenly it seemed, Galway Bay opened out to the left, with Lough Corrib on the right like an inland sea.

Galway is now a large town, not industrialized but much extended into suburbs. In the narrow central streets a few carved doorways and Spanishy arches remain, but the old houses of the Claddagh, the fishermen's quarter, have almost all been replaced by modern cottages.

To the west, across the Claddagh Bridge, this district retained its native Irish laws for centuries – its own king even, for in spite of repressive measures it resisted at heart the domination of the Twelve Tribes of Galway. These Anglo-Norman settlers sought to impose an alien rule on Connemara: 'neither O nor Mac shall strutte ne swagger in the streets of Galway', as a statute in the Corporation Book of the town decreed. Restrictions were even imposed to limit the traditional Gaelic hospitality, and those who regard the oppression of the Celtic peoples as a figment of paranoic fancy should study these and similar documents. In Ireland, between the political tyranny of the English and the puritanical tyranny of the Catholic Church, it is a wonder that even the echo of a Gaelic heritage can still be heard.

The Claddagh clung to its ancient ways, safeguarding fragments at least of its own culture in language, institutions and skills. The design of the Claddagh wedding ring, two hands clasping a heart, is famous, but the original rings, heavy and of rough gold, are scarcely imitated by the flimsy examples displayed in jewellers' shops today. I remember that I nearly chose one of these for my wedding ring, but the jeweller candidly advised against it, saying it would not wear well. As things happened, it would have proved a more appropriate symbol than the solid-gold buckle that I selected instead, which has long outlasted what it betokened.

On the mainland, the people's picturesque clothes have disappeared almost everywhere except for an occasional black shawleen. But a woman from the Aran Islands stood out in contrast to the Galway citizens on the crowded pavement by her free and noble bearing, the red-gold hair looped about her ears, the full striped skirt and the dark shawl held as a sling to carry her baby. The prophecy 'Athenry was, Galway is, Aran shall be the best of the three' perhaps applies to costume. Hers was the type of Gaelic peasant that, carried over into the dispossessed tinker tribes, has been perpetuated in the women of Augustus John, who modelled them upon it. The *tenue* was once fashionable in the art world but, now long outmoded, is followed only by obscure groups in Cornwall perhaps.

After some tea at Salthill, Galway's seaside resort, which we drank overlooking the bay, still and blue under a warm sun, we started to climb into the hills of Connacht. B.Z. was looking over to our right with apprehensive nostalgia, for we should be passing near Rosscahill, her old home, abandoned at the time of 'the troubles'. Soon it came into view, the house standing solidly above the tranquil lake as she remembered it and the woods, which she feared would have been felled, still growing down to the water's edge. Though accidentally burned some years ago, the house had been rebuilt much as before, square and grey. If, as some assert, it was ancestral spirits who set the place ablaze, resenting a stranger's intrusion after so many centuries, then they must have been pacified since by this continuity of style. The place is now owned by an Englishman, who has become more Irish than the Irish in the country of his adoption, wearing the saffron kilt and greeting visitors with a flow of Gaelic.

But if the house and the grounds immediately surrounding it seemed hardly changed, the outlying parts of the demesne, which had been sold separately, were neglected; what had once been the main avenue had fallen into decay; urns were missing from the entrance pillars, and coping had slipped from the walls.

The weather was growing clearer and more golden with every mile further west. The road surface had been deteriorating since we left Galway town, and once we had passed Oughterard, with its strange shelves of rock overhanging the salmon river and supporting a row of stiff-trunked saplings, it grew narrow, pitted and twisting. The Twelve Pins, or rather Bens, Connemara's dominant mountain mass, rose up before us, partly screened by the eastern cones of the Maamturk range reflected in a chain of loughs, their surface level as glass. Across miles of mulberry-dark bogland we drove towards them, the tawny of king ferns lining the ditches that bordered the road. Air of a wonderful transparency arched above us, blue washed with white gold. I did not regret our slow pace, enforced by the pot-holes in the road, since I could watch the mountains from gradually shifting angles.

After bearing to the left once or twice, we suddenly saw that the sheet of water ahead was not another lough but a long inlet of the sea – Bertraghboy Bay – and we caught sight of Roundstone's church tower standing distantly on its margin. We had been told, optimistically, that it was sixty miles from Athlone, but we must have come at least that distance from Galway. Since morning we had touched the counties of Dublin, Kildare, Meath, Westmeath, Roscommon and Galway. At last we were turning into the avenue through the woods of Letterdyfe.

Before dinner, J. and I had time for a quick bathe in the white-sanded creek of Erraloch, set some three miles beyond Roundstone village in landscape not unlike that of the Scilly Islands, though vaster – the same huge granity boulders and translucent sea.

Later in the evening we again drove out westward beyond Ballyconneely. To the left, a desolate coastline, much indented;

to the right, the mass of Errisbeg and the 365 loughs that are said to be visible from its summit; ahead, the sun sinking, a sanguine globe, to extinguish itself in a band of mist above the sea. We returned in the falling dusk.

Letterdyfe

NEXT DAY THE weather was again fine and warm, so J. and I drove to Erraloch to have another bathe. A track serving a few small houses skirted the tiny oblong creek; to the right a stone jetty like a ramp was thrust into the green water, where cattle were wading to escape the flies. Seaward loomed the outline of Inishlackan; inland, the bastions of Errisbeg.

We took the track to the left, and, scrambling over rocks to a place where the water was deeper than that of the inlet itself, we plunged into its icy embrace. No more than a brief swim would be enjoyable in that cold sea. Afterwards we hailed a boatman who said he was going to Roundstone harbour and would take us for the trip. His turf-boat, with a new outboard motor, drew against some flattish rocks, and we sprang in. We chugged away from the shore and were soon following the navigable channel that left the island of Inishlackan to port and rounding a promontory with the grey convent buildings of the Franciscans to starboard.

We asked the boatman if he liked living here? No, if he had his choice he would be living at Kingston, Surrey. J. wanted to bathe from the boat and be towed along on a rope, but the boatman did not encourage him in this. We asked if he ever bathed? No, he had enough salt water anyhow without that, he said.

We coasted beside the straggling village of Roundstone that culminates, architecturally if not spiritually, in the square tower of the Church of Ireland – a landmark for miles around – then slowed down and entered the harbour. This was quite large and had the air of having once known busier times than at present. Indeed, with those harbours southward, Casheen and Kilkieran, it was said to be the only one between the Shannon and Lough Swilly that could take ships of any size, though this is difficult to reconcile with the fact that Killary Harbour could hold the British fleet. The boatman tied up against the stone steps, and, while he was in the village on his 'messages', we sat in the boat sunning ourselves, sheltered by the depth of the black harbour walls. Presently he came back with a sack of flour and several other packages, and we returned to Erraloch over the smooth water.

J. had to drive back to Dublin, so he set out on his journey about noon. I bathed again in the evening from the tiny strand below Letterdyfe, rocky and weedy though it was. Then I turned to face the Twelve Bens, which inevitably focus the eyes in these parts. Their Irish name is Beanna Beola, Beola's Bens, called after the giant Beola who was said to have been a Firbolg chieftain ruling the region they dominate. Now, himself dominated, he lay interred beneath these monstrous tombstones. Seen from Letterdyfe, the contour of Derryclare Mountain certainly took on the likeness of a huge recumbent figure – the Crusader, C. called him, the distant precipices seeming to encase in sculptured armour a stiff body below. How like and yet different is that neighbour of Mount Errigal, Aghlamore in Donegal, a mountain not less bare and wild than these of Connemara but which, moulded perhaps by glacial attrition, suggests by its rounder forms the effigy of a sleeping giantess.

A faint tang of burning turf hung in the air like that of fried bacon; this is the smell that most vividly evokes Ireland for me, calling up a picture of three conical forms: the maroon-coloured stack of turf, the white gable-end of a cabin, the blue pyramid of a hill. In this region the cutting, drying, stacking of turf from the bogs is still done by hand and goes on during most of the summer months. In some other places, however, the industry was much expanded through various mechanical methods during the war, when coal was almost unobtainable. Now the country ranks second only to the Soviet Union as a producer of turf for fuel.

I began to wander along the road that skirts the shore of Bertraghboy Bay; the tide being low, just at the turn, had left uncovered the estuary banks of dark mud brought down through the ages by the Owenmore River from Ballynahinch. A thin scum, debris of a vast inlet, was lying stagnant in the creeks on the surface of this outflow, which seemed to breathe, heaving with an almost extinguished impulse from waves of the open sea.

I remembered how purposefully the tide would flow at evening into Dingle Bay with the Blasket Islands sometimes visible to the west, under a gash of burnished brass torn in the storm clouds above the Dingle Peninsula. The Blaskets have now joined the many deserted islands off Ireland's coast; for their last inhabitants, unable any longer to endure the severity of conditions there, were recently evacuated to the mainland.

A penetrating cry, often repeated like that of a cricket but louder, came from the grass in the small fields set aside for hay. Watching for a moment I saw the russet body of a corn-crake scud over the silky tips of the mowing-grass on wings that seemed scarcely strong enough to carry it and sink down where the growth was deepest.

Now a sudden wind sprang up from northward, drawing a curtain of grey across the Twelve Bens and obscuring their noble mass. Next morning this veil, thinning out from their summits, covered the whole sky and dissipated the sun's warmth. A chilly breeze blew, which made the sea uninviting; but it was possible to sunbathe nude in a sheltered place, and I found one in the 'wild garden', an overgrown rockery. Here I was screened from the wind by a tangle of plants – foxgloves, ferns, ragged robin, small hazel bushes, furze, rushes and brambles – and captured for an hour or so, hidden in fragrant vegetation, almost the atmosphere of *L'Après-midi d'un Faune.* The most searching wind seemed to pass by this nook without entering, and I often came here afterwards, sometimes even when a light rain was falling. Few sensations excel in delicacy the *pétillement* of minute raindrops tingling over the whole surface of the skin, warmed at the same time by a silvery sun.

In the woods of Letterdyfe I discovered what looked like an ancient burial chamber. In this broken mound, the association of stone slabs, some now recumbent but others still standing to form a roughly rectangular cist, with quartzite pebbles about the size of a cricket ball, suggested a Bronze Age barrow. Long ago the capstone must have been removed and the contents rifled; now all was moss-grown under the evergreen shade. A second eminence a few yards away might also have been a tumulus, but it was so covered with rubble and overgrown by brambles that I could not be certain. Small round-barrows like these are often the remains of a late-neolithic or Bronze Age cemetery, so Letterdyfe may have been built on a site that had been occupied, by living or dead, for thousands of years.

In the late evening I showed my find to C. and E. who ran the guest-house. They had no idea that the property contained antiquities, though E. had lived here all her life, her father having been agent to the Ballynahinch estate. He had built Letterdyfe House, designing it with the Victorian virtues of solidity and comfort. It must be one of the few country houses in Ireland that are warm and dry; it is certainly the only one I have come across. I have heard tales of a certain 'place' in County Cork where the sea came in at the drawing-room windows during high tides. And elsewhere I have myself found red sandals grown green with mould when I came to pack them after a short stay, during which they were unused because only the thickest boots were necessary. But Letterdyfe even seems to be centrally heated, though this, in fact, is not so – only it is so well sited under a sheltering spur of Errisbeg and embedded in coniferous woods that the worst winds are broken and leave it untouched.

A path turning off the avenue led through the vegetable gardens, parts of which were untended and overgrown with iris-like plants. One evening I wandered through these to the hillside beyond, covered with rhododendron bushes now flowering in all shades of magenta, where cuckoos called all day and far into the night. There is nothing pleasanter, should the weather be kind, than to lie on such a hillside in the hollow behind a rock or in a nook of the half-tropical shrubbery and gaze at the foreground of heathland and scattered boulders. Where better can one indulge the longing for tranquillity, for no mechanical noise will break the peace of bog and sky, and even a passing aeroplane is a rarity. The Gaelic word *suaimhneas* expresses this luxuriating in quiet. But all too often damp soaks up through the mossy ground or a keen gust makes one shiver, and the trance is broken. If only the climate were more clement, what a paradise this country would be! But the wet is said to make the intense green of the grass, the lushness of leafage in localities with a good soil and the luxuriance of certain trees and shrubs even in mountainy districts such as this, where the soil is almost too poor for grazing.

A bell rang faintly over the mile or so of bogland that lay under the slopes of Errisbeg, between Roundstone and Letterdyfe. Whatever the local vagaries of summertime, the angelus follows the sun and so was sounded at this time of year, at one o'clock for midday and at seven in the evening.

Before the sounding of that first Christian bell, which was to restore their human shape to the swan-children of Lir, there was no history in Ireland because there was no writing. Ogham was never used, as far as is known, to classify events; it was the entrance of the Latin alphabet and script which brought the beginnings of mundane chronicle. Before the convent bell divided day and night into regular hours, there was no time – none, that is, in the Western sense of a guilt-ridden urgency. There was no need for written history, because past and present were not sharply distinguished and man could enter the ever-present record if need be, since all veils were thin. One with his race, whether living or dead, he still retained kinship with supernatural races.

Measuring time by stars, sun and moon, he had no need of clocks. For public undertakings, he sought the auspicious moment, discovered for him by Druids using their trained faculties of intuition. For private meetings or transactions, he relied on similar, if less developed, powers within himself. In this, more than anything else, does pagan innocence and happiness consist that man is unsubjected to the tyranny of time.

Ancient Ireland also proved that a civilization can thrive independent of towns. Even today, large urban centres are few and are situated without exception on the coastal periphery. None of them were of Gaelic foundation, all being imposed on Gaeldom from without by Skand, Saxon or Anglo-Norman. Even a village on the Saxon model, with dwellings centred around a church, is uncharacteristic here, where the isolated holding or the scattered hamlet called the town-land is more typical. The word anglicized as bally in many place-names is the Irish *baile* meaning not town, as often translated, but the very different concept of the town-land.

This decentralized ideal was refracted back and forth between building and institution. The intensely personal working of even modern officialdom recalls those distant ages when law was enforced, not by the state but by individual jurists with the numen of Druidic tradition behind them. It is the echo of this past life, timeless and unurbanized, that refreshes one still in the Ireland of today.

The same is true of all Celtic countries, in so far as the same causes operate. The past is present in the holy unconscious, and in regions not yet entirely divorced from it essential care is not for ambition and the rationalized outlook. The sense of individual identity is softened, the ego tending to sink and be engulfed in the id. Achievement scarcely counts; existence in relation to the moment is all. No wonder that time loses its anxiety or, rather, has never reached the anxious pitch; the angles of space, also bathed in an age-old ambience, leave aside their sharpness.

Out of this background comes the Irish 'evasiveness', 'blarney', 'never giving a straight answer', as the English say. If the Irishman does not answer directly it is because he does not like questions, particularly questions of a factual character – 'How many miles to So-and-So?', 'What time does the post go/the bus come?', etc. Not primarily concerned with time and distance, his focus is otherwhere; questions of fact worry him, and he answers vaguely, jokingly, 'untruthfully' or with pointless flattery. To him, interrogation is not conversation (which he loves), and he will escape it if he can. Desiring a living relationship, he resents being used as a means to an end.

But one should enter a country such as this as if it were the embodiment of some profounder level of one's own being, spread out before one and inviting one to wander. To some, what they find may be disagreeable; to others, it is a delight; to others again, it is both and neither – it exists and therefore is accepted. These countries have a penetrable quality which others do not possess, unless it be those of the Orient Tracks that lead nowhere, people without aim other than their intrinsic being – perhaps Ireland shares these with the East, like some of the patterns of her illuminated manuscripts. But there is none of the dazzling, the appalling, the relentless quality of the Orient. The 'new' Ireland, the 'new' India may be trying to Europeanize or Americanize themselves, but how long are the changes brought about by this process to last? For how long may the *genius loci* be defied?

In Europe, the atmosphere of opening is best felt, I think, in lands where there is little to westward: Penwith at this season was my first experience of it. I saw that nothing could perish in that douce air, where all reflected silver to the sky, and I desired nothing but to wander onwards over soil and stone, existing in relation to the thrift and navelwort in bloom along the cliffs and the calm beginning of the Atlantic below me.

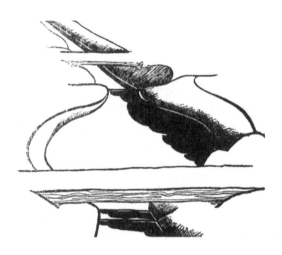

Roundstone

N<small>O ONE CAN</small> be long in Roundstone without wanting to visit Inishnee, so one morning I crossed the rusting bridge that joined it to the mainland and followed its only road. The island was almost without trees, scanty bushes cowering only beside the whitewashed dwellings.

Though they were connected to the coast of the bay, the people retained an islander's attitude and regarded a stranger as an entertaining event. All seemed ready to talk, especially about Letterdyfe, telling me that E was 'a beautiful lady'. The aura of long residence hung about her in their minds, linking them to the days when her father was agent at Ballynahinch.

At one house a gypsy-faced woman with a young daughter called out to me, 'Do you love geese?'

I could not believe my ears.

'Do you love geese?' she repeated.

'No, I'm afraid of them,' I replied. She had driven hers, I was thankful to see, into a stone pen.

'They want to go away on the tide,' she told me, 'and if they do, it's hard to get them again.' So she would not let them out. The weather worsened, and the strong wind hurled lashings of rain at me. I tried to draw, but the gusts tore at my pages, making them flutter like a flag, and spattered on the lines of ink, producing lovely effects that I did not intend. Soon my fingers became too numb to work, and I decided to explore the island another day.

I went back to Letterdyfe and had a talk with John the gardener and general handyman, without whom the establishment could scarcely have been carried on. Though lame, he managed to do most of the outdoor jobs and could even peddle his bicycle with one foot. He told me that almost the only time to see the traditional dress was on fair days which usually coincided with some festival of the church such as that of St Peter and St Paul, the Assumption or the Birthday of the Virgin. He was digging the light soil with the long-handled spade called a loy, the equivalent of which I have seen used in Cornwall and the Scillies.

I had noticed only one Roundstone man wearing the crios, a girdle of plaited wool in brilliant colours to hold a wrapped-over jacket, but his was so darkened with grime as to be almost unrecognizable. The Galway of the red petticoats is a thing of the past, and the villages are dimmer for their disappearance. They were still worn in the remoter parts of Donegal when I first visited these, but may have gone from there also by now.

Unless one is satisfied with the uninviting strand below Letterdyfe, one must go some distance for a bathe. On a fine morning, with the inevitable chilly wind, I set out for the nearest cove beyond the village, that beside the Franciscan monastery. Mr H. gave me a lift as far as the turning, and one of the brothers, who was painting the massive wrought-iron gates of their avenue, gave me directions. I took a path across some hayfields, where the flowering grasses stood thick with other flowers, the red bloom of sorrel over all. Here I met two more members of the community carrying between them a heavy bucket from the well. One of them, a young boy in ordinary clothes, seemed to have taken a vow of silence or else to be very shy, but the other, who was wearing a robe, answered my question about the cove.

To the left of the meadows a high wall surrounded the convent precinct; but in Ireland no wall is so forbidding as to be without a gap, and this I soon found. Peering through it I saw the chalky glint of a figure of the Sacred Heart among the shrubs of the garden, its flaking plaster standing against sea spray and breeze. Such statues, like the crosses on the Wicklow heights, struggle vainly to subdue unchristened nature, where elements tirelessly wear them down.

Following the slope of the fields almost as far as the sea, I came upon the well whence the bucket had been filled. It made the lower end of the field marshy, but I avoided the morass, and, climbing over a wall on the edge of a low cliff, I dropped down to a tiny arc of sand. I waded about for some time in the translucent shallows before I could summon the courage to immerse myself completely.

By these unfrequented strands one may occasionally catch sight of a seal. They were once more numerous, perhaps, for the name of Roundstone, though it has been derived from *Cuan na cloice runta*, may be from Cloch-an-Rón, the Stone of the Seal – the Anglicized version, like many more, being a mistranslation based on a pun or similarity of sound. The Gaelic revival has done much to arrest such vitiation of the native culture.

As I walked back through the village I stopped to buy something at Julia's, one of the several general shops which were also bars. The customary layout for the more prosperous of these shops is a wide passage between two counters, one selling groceries or drapery or both, the other drinks. N.V. was there, and we had a few gins together. This habit certainly eases the boredom of shopping and might well be adopted in England.

I told Julia I wanted to go to Croagh Patrick, Ireland's holy mountain in County Mayo where she came from, and then she began telling me about the pilgrimages to Knock. This is Cnoc Mhuire in Irish, Mary's Hill, the site of one of the Virgin's later appearances. This took place on 21 August 1879, not very distant in time from the vision of Bernadette at Lourdes. It was seen simultaneously by fifteen people of all ages, the Virgin's figure, with those of St Joseph, St John the Evangelist and the Lamb of God, palely gleaming below the gable-end of the church in the rainy twilight. The ground below remained dry, a phenomenon paralleled by the unwetting shower at Fátima. One woman stated that when she first noticed the figures she took them to be statues, which makes one think that what she saw was in monochrome – coloured statues would hardly be placed on the exterior of a small grey church without protection from the elements. Perhaps, of those who see visions, the majority do not register colour, and some described by St Teresa of Ávila tend to confirm this. It has been estimated that some 75 per cent of humanity never dreams in colour.

The fame of Knock spread rapidly. An altar with a canopy was built over the spot, and mass is celebrated in the open air. Outdoor ritual often retains something of vagabond spontaneity and can scarcely grow stuffy and over-respectable. Crowds come from all over Ireland and beyond, the first contingent from America arriving in 1949. The Assumption is the chief day of pilgrimage, but each Sunday throughout the summer the shrine is thronged, cures of the sick and other favours being attributed to it.

The Knock Shrine Annual, given me by Julia in the hope of converting me, reported a number of these. Apparently the clients of Our Lady of Knock can obtain almost anything they want, be it recovery from illness, fertility, safe confinement, success in examinations, monetary help, suitable employment or a marriage partner. The following quotation is typical of many:

> I prayed fervently to Our Lady of Knock that an operation for a malignant growth would be a complete success, and I also made a pilgrimage to her shrine for this intention. Several X-rays were taken since the operation, and now the doctors tell me I am completely better. I also want to thank Our Lady of Knock for saving my turkeys after they had got some kind of disease. Only one died. My heart's gratitude for the kind intercession of Our Lady of Knock in all my needs.

Though one may be inclined to smile at the turkeys with their somewhat ill-defined malady, it would be rash to dismiss all such testimony as the result of suggestion, hysteria, the vagaries of journalism or deliberate fraud. With Christian apparitions and their results, one is in the realm of the marvellous, equally with the phenomena of spiritism and with flying saucers. In all there remains, after discounting everything that can be discounted, an irreducible minimum of cases for which common-sense explanation is inadequate.

Aesthetically, one may feel that the heterogeneous group in the Knock apparition is inferior to the dignity of the Lady whose single figure dominated Lourdes. The Mayo shrine still lacks recognition by papal authority, and the caution of the Vatican in accepting such visions is understandable. Only two months after my talk with Julia, the *Daily Mirror* published the story of a similar vision at Arboe in Tyrone, in which six people claimed to have seen the Virgin. But there is no doubt that Catholic Ireland already regards Cnoc Mhuire as her own equivalent of Fátima or La Salette.

Another day Mr H. and his son took me to Gorteen Strand for a bathe. The turning for this lies further along the coast road to Ballyconneely and Clifden than that leading to Erraloch. When one has passed the boulder-strewn country that lies between the main road and the sea, an immense crescent of white sand backed by dunes and filled with pellucid water reflecting the sky in a deeper shade lies before one. As usual a keen wind made bathing a Spartan exercise, but we plunged in all the same.

This country, wild and bleak though it was, had not the terrifying vastness of the Kerry coast where the long strand of Rossbeigh stretched across the head of the Dingle inlet. There I once made a line drawing with a stick in the sand of a landscape which must have covered nearly an acre, echoing the range of mountains that ran out towards Valentia Island.

When I first caught sight of Seefin, just inland, I exclaimed, 'That mountain is full of demons!'

On the return we met some tinkers, their carts, covered with the traditional rounded hood, being carved and gaily painted in red and yellow. Their lean horses, at least two to each cart, one drawing it and one following loose behind, looked as wild as their owners. Tinkers are not usually true gypsies, who are dark-skinned, but tend to be blond or reddish. Their fine features and beauty of bearing give colour to the theory that they are the last strays of Gaeldom's aristocracy, dispossessed by a succession of conquerors, Elizabethan, Cromwellian and later. An aura of romance invests their shawled women and shock-headed boys; their poverty does not extinguish the picturesqueness of their clothes, their entire appearance giving the lie to the doctrine of glossy magazines, that 'beauty' and good grooming are inseparable. With them, beauty thrives alongside untidiness and filth and must be beauty indeed to rise above vermin. They are some of the few free people in a regimented world, though their liberty is bought at the price of the lowest living standards.

Settled people dislike and distrust the tinkers. One day I saw a woman with the unmistakable nomad gait, a brown check shawl draped around her and a barefoot boy in clothes much too big for him running at her heels. She was watched suspiciously from every open doorway giving on to Roundstone Street, and harsh looks followed her even after she had vanished up the hill.

Going through Roundstone, one could not help passing the deadest of its houses, the Church of Ireland rectory. So long shut up that it was impossible even to let, it stood forlornly above a steep avenue overgrown with weeds and mosses, the approach barred by a locked gate. The trees had been taken over completely by a colony of rooks, whose droppings bespattered all beneath. So jealous were they of their domain that they resented with strident cries even the pausing of a passer-by on the road below. There was evidently too little demand for the services of a cleric to justify his residence.

At sunset that evening there were wonderful colours in mountain and cloud, strange fulvous pinks and lichenous yellows against a clear, warm-tinted sky with a few of those pencil lines that often presage rain. But with the fall of evening it grew intensely cold; by the feel of the air it might be January, and indeed local people said that there was little seasonal change. But if the Twelve Bens and all the Connemara mountains of comparable height were snow-covered – and I have no doubt they often are, having seen their compeers so, northward in Donegal and southward in Kerry – the wind would have a still-keener edge. I had long ceased to trust the patriot who tells one that Ireland is a warm place; I know that it seldom is for long, at any season. In general, the weather is either very wet and misty – 'a soft day, thank God' – or very cold, with a north-east wind if fine. My 'summer' *tenue* consisted of wool vest and ski pants, wool socks, trousers, sweater, scarf and poncho, fur jacket and fleece-lined boots. I recommend trousers (though public opinion in many places is still against them for women) because ski pants can be worn under them, and hand-knit socks are warmer than nylons.

The rigours and uncertainty of the climate may be responsible for the fact that, though Ireland must be one of the most inspiring countries to the *paysagiste*, it has never been adequately represented in paint. Jack Yeats has come nearer to it than any other artist, but the scope of his work is wider than landscape. It is difficult to imagine a country with such subtle atmospheric variations, such individual colour, such variety of form in small compass. If I were primarily a landscape painter, I would try to ignore the discomforts, if only for the sunsets; as Turner said, 'The sun never sets so beautifully as in Ireland.'

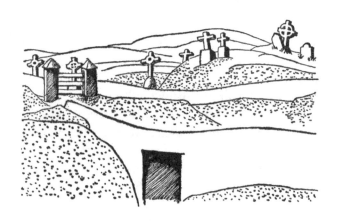

Croagh Patrick

S TANLEY CALLED FOR me in the morning – rather late, on account of a visit to a garage – and we drove through Ballyconneely, leaving on our left the low-lying promontory that sharpens to Slyne Head. On the way to Errislannan we skirted Mannin Bay, called after Manannán Mac Lir who also gave his name to the Isle of Man, Mannan beg Mac y Leir being the Manx equivalent. If Lir is the Gaelic Oceanus, then Manannán is Nereus or Poseidon; and Shakespeare's *King Lear* owes something of his elemental force to descent from an elemental deity.

The Errislannan peninsula is one of the least-frequented districts of Connemara, a poor road adding to its inaccessibility. It is out of the way for visitors going to Clifden or Roundstone, and they usually pass it by. Its name derives from St Flannan, patron of its parish of Ballindoon, who is also commemorated by the remote Flannan Isles beyond the Outer Hebrides. A haunting poem by Wilfrid Wilson Gibson described how in the year 1900 the Seven Hunters' Lighthouse was found empty, the three keepers due to be relieved having vanished without trace.

> Like curs a glance has brought to heel
> We listened, flinching there:
> And looked and looked on the untouched meal
> And the overtoppled chair.
>
> We seemed to stand for an endless while
> Though still no word was said,

> Three men alive on Flannan Isle
> Who thought on three men dead.

The mystery of their fate was never solved.

There used to be a legend that no one must be buried in the graveyard of Kilflannan or the body would appear next day on the surface of the ground. (These inhospitable cemeteries were not uncommon in Connacht, though it is difficult to say what could have given rise to their reputation.) But this one is still in demand as a last resting place, for it was opened again about twenty years ago after a long period of disuse. It had remained enclosed in the wooded demesne of Errislannan Manor, and a deputation of the local people persuaded the uncomprehending owners of the property to allow interments there once again. But no church of St Flannan remains, and it is the Church of Ireland building which dominates the peninsula, poised on its highest point opposite the entrance to Drinagh.

Stanley and Sally were staying in a ramshackle lodge on the demesne, approached by an avenue twisting through scrub silvered by lichen – furze bushes, small trees bent over by the wind and shrubs of the pittosporum – the type of low-growing tangled woodland found in the shallow valleys of west Cornwall. The house itself had once been solidly built but had been allowed to fall into disrepair, so it was draughty and full of rat holes. Needless to say, a coat of paint was long overdue. There were gaping cracks in the walls of the lavatory, the beds seemed ready to collapse if one lay on them; the large gilt mirror above the sitting-room hearth was falling to pieces, while unreadable books mouldered in the shelves. But the place was charmingly situated, the back windows looking down a ferny slope to that arm of the sea which makes Errislannan almost an island. At lunch we had a kind of cream jelly made of the carrageen moss of which I am particularly fond. This is a seaweed that grows on rocks just below high-water level, and the jelly is delicious when flavoured with lemon juice. It has a high reputation as a specific in chest complaints, and I can vouch for its efficacy in bronchitis, having lived on it for several days when ill in a Kerry cottage.

We started for Croagh Patrick along the rough road down the peninsula and then turned left into Clifden, the 'capital' of Connemara. The monthly market was transferred here from Ballinaboy in Errislannan, which must have declined in importance. Here *resheen*, the red cloth teased with honey, could still be bought and the Breedeen, a kind of tweed made by combining the bleached with the unbleached wool as weft and warp. As in many another country town, the ornamental typefaces of last century were popular as lettering for shop-fronts, and the free use of colour on buildings imparted to them a meridional air, too often belied, alas, by the climate. In Ireland, a butcher's shop is often labelled a victualler; a chemist's a medical hall.

We traversed the desolate moorlands of Streamstown and reached Letterfrack, above which the pyramid of Diamond Mountain stood out from the mist-filled chasms of the Twelve Bens' northern face. Away to the left, across Ballynakill Harbour, lay the Renvyle promontory with its steep rounded hill. In this landscape, the small houses with white- or colour-washed walls looked appropriate, though the thatched roof which is part of the same tradition was fast giving way to slate or, worse, galvanized iron. Even so, a smoke-blue wash on the plaster walls can look charming combined, as it often was, with blood-red paint on the woodwork. And white walls may be enlivened with sea green or jaded rose colour in their window recesses.

Next we caught sight of the Victorian battlements of Kylemore Abbey, the wooded wall of Doughruagh rising behind. Kylemore was built last century by a wealthy businessman as a residence for himself but is now a convent school and guest-house. Soon we were running along the shore of Killary Harbour, with haunted Muilrea, the Bald King, rising sheer from its opposite bank. The water of this fjord-like inlet was marked by a thread of foam running like a marble vein up the centre as far as the fishing hamlet of Leenane, that faced the vast cone of Bengorm.

We were over the Mayo border, the weather growing greyer as we made our way further north. Much of Galway benefits from the shelter of successive mountain ranges – Maamturk, Muilrea, Partry and Sheefry, to say nothing of the Twelve Bens – which protect it from the north and west.

Our road now took a long downwards slope across bogland, which should have given us a fine view of Croagh Patrick's isolated ridge, but almost the whole mountain was enveloped in mist. *Croagh*, *cruagh* or *cruach* is any high hill like a stack.

We turned left just before the town of Westport and took the coast road, with Clew Bay on our right and the mountain to our left, stopping a little later to buy fruit and sweets. We heard about the pilgrimage from the fey-looking woman who served us and had taken part in it many times. Her dark-green eyes darted from one to another as she told us about it.

One climbs to the Reek, as she called Croagh Patrick, on Garland Sunday, the last in July. Some go up without shoes, their feet becoming lacerated long before they reach the top by the sharp stones and slivers of Connemara marble which make up the 'path'. The last part of this is little better than a scree. In the church on the summit, masses are said from earliest dawn, so pilgrims start the ascent at midnight or before. Those who intend to 'receive', climb fasting; those who wish to make a special penance crawl part of the way on hands and knees. Some distance up, we were told, is a group of three carns, and the pilgrim walks seven times around each one, reciting seven 'Paters' the while; there are similar peregrinations to be made at the top. This is perhaps the most striking instance of the turrus, a remnant of nature worship surviving to this day under a Christian cloak, though it is difficult to say whether it attracts a greater number of devotees than St Patrick's Purgatory in Lough Derg. This latter pilgrimage, if less strenuous, is more exacting, for it lasts three days during which food and sleep are strictly rationed.

To others, the climbing of the Reek is more in the nature of an expedition, and these make the ascent with a stout stick in one hand and a bottle of whiskey in the other. Many are not Catholics and undertake the 2,500-foot climb as an expression of national solidarity rather than as a religious exercise.

Rain often falls heavily during the whole journey, and on the summit, which is seldom without its veil of mist, the cold is bitter in the early hours. But it is claimed by the faithful that none ever caught a cold on the pilgrimage, and, though ambulances are in attendance at the starting points, stretcher cases are said to be few. (The more sceptical employers, however, complain of much absenteeism consequent upon the Reek, and of illness directly attributable to exhaustion and exposure.) At the foot, stalls selling refreshments do a good trade, for upwards of 70,000 people converge here on the appointed day. It is a Western equivalent – more rigorous if less colourful – of the Paraheira procession in honour of the Buddha on the mountain top near Kandy in Ceylon.

What is the origin of the vast assembly? The date of it alone would make one suspect a pre-Christian origin, being evidently transferred from 2 August, Lughnasadh, one of the four festivals of the Gaelic year. This name commemorates the marriage of Lugh, god of light, with Ériu, a personification of Ireland herself. The Christian version is that St Patrick fasted for forty days on the mountain top as a prelude to his banishment of snakes, toads and suchlike vermin from the country. He cast his exorcizing bell down the slopes after them, from which it was kindly retrieved for him by an angel, till none remained alive. Nor is this legend wholly phantastic, if one agrees with Seamus MacCall in *And So Began the Irish Nation*, that not actual snakes but their images and other cult objects belonging to serpent worship were overthrown. The spectacular shape and isolated position of the hill must have marked it out as a pagan sanctuary long before it was a Christian one. There have never been snakes in Ireland, as geological evidence proves, but there are traces of a snake cult in early times. Serpent forms can be found in neolithic rock scribings; and the name of the celebrated image Crom Cruach, who was a kind of Gaelic Moloch, suggests that it may have been a snake-mound like the one near Kilmartin in Argyllshire.

In the neighbourhood of the holy mountain are to be found St Patrick's Stone, an obvious megalith, and, in the other direction, St Patrick's Well, situated in a limbo-graveyard. St Patrick is thus a comparatively modern name for a locally presiding divinity.

Such limbo-graveyards are frequently to be found in Ireland, suggesting that the people have always been attached to that grim dogma which excludes unbaptized infants from heaven.

Recently, a distinguished Jesuit whose kindness of heart seems to equal his learning has set out, in *The Downside Quarterly*, to discover whether this doctrine may not be modified without heresy. It is noteworthy that while he was successful in adducing a number of liberal interpretations from other countries, his Irish authorities came down strongly in favour of the traditional view. Limbo-graveyards are often situated on the cemeteries of pagans, whose earthly paradise, or 'natural happiness', the blameless unbaptized are said to share.

Further down the road we stopped at a guest-house for some tea before taking a closer look at the mountain. We had a long wait while the brown soda bread was baking in the oven; even when it arrived it was only half done and very doughy.

But our hostess regaled us with stories of Gráinne Uaile, or Grace O'Malley, still remembered in these parts as a legendary figure. She belonged to that type of warrior-queen which Celtic civilization cast up in Maeve of Connacht and Boadicea and could still produce before entirely subjected to an alien ethos. Gráinne ruled Mayo and the Western Isles for many years, during which her exploits at sea made her famous. This saucy Amazon had two husbands at least and lovers by the score; on one occasion she visited Elizabeth I, who for once appears to have been nonplussed. In desperation she offered her the title of countess, but Gráinne haughtily refused the honour, saying that she was a queen already.

Looking over Clew Bay, we could see westward the cliffs of Clare Island, the stronghold from which she dominated this sea, black-green now, flecked with white and scattered over with bleak humped islets of a different green as far as the eye could reach. It is called 'the bay of a thousand isles', though there are said to be 365 of them, one for each day of the year.

By the time we found the beginning of the Way to the Clouds, the evening had grown yet more misty and a light rain was falling. The local Civic Guard was alarmed that we should try the ascent, and, in fact, we only reached the first statue of St Patrick. The white figure showed stains of the rusting armature below, and the plaster was peeling off the stem of the crozier. The pedestal was roughly decorated with patterns incised while the concrete was still wet and afterwards daubed with green paint. Each face showed a variant of the shamrock motif – a plant associated with the Beltane celebrations which St Patrick, by lighting the paschal fire on the Hill of Slane, is said to have taken over for Christianity. The thread-like lines on the north-eastern face maintained almost the proportions of the Tree of Life, the slot for offerings occupying the place of Daath.

We hurried down the track again, and, crossing the road,

glanced at the ruins of Murrisk Abbey. The rain had become so heavy that we were not tempted to linger but went on to Old Head, near Louisburgh, for the night. The approach to the hotel above a desolate beach had an air of neglect, but the place proved to be modern and well run.

Next morning the proprietor told us about Caher, an island off the Mayo coast with a reputation for past sanctity. But the famed monastic settlement seemed to have been hurriedly abandoned, for when he visited it extinguished candles still guttered on the altar of the church.

In his opinion, the most isolated places in Ireland were to be found in north Mayo; one hamlet he knew there was only accessible by the weekly post van. (Some, but apparently not all, Irish post vans have a notice fixed to the windscreen saying that passengers are prohibited.) He could not return by the same conveyance, since its few seats had been booked weeks ahead. He was faced with a choice between a twenty-seven-mile tramp through the mountains to the nearest bus and a scramble across extensive quicksands, with the ferryman's daughter as guide, followed by a walk of fifteen miles. He took a risk on the girl and the quicksands.

The next morning was still wet and misty, the summit of Croagh Patrick still obscured by cloud. We drove back by Louisburgh village, beyond which we paused to look at a standing-stone near the road, then on to the dark expanse of Doolough, from which rise sheer the northern walls of Muilrea. Passing Delphi, which may have been named for a fancied resemblance to the country around the ancient shrine – though I could see none – we again approached Leenane, this time from the other side of Killary Harbour. As we stopped there for a drink at a bar, the name of MacBride on a small shop reminded us that Maude Gonne's husband came from here.

The weather brightened as we re-entered Galway, and we arrived back at Errislannan for a very late lunch.

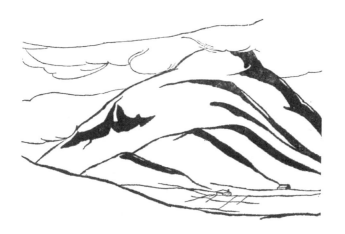

Round-Tower and West Cross, Monasterboice

Tobar Breanainn

THE ISLAND OF Inishnee stretched along the haven of Bertraghboy parallel with the coasts, dividing it into Blackford on the east and Roundstone on the west, to which bank it is connected. The water of the deep and narrow channel thus spanned ran swiftly at certain states of the tide.

There always seemed to be a gale blowing as one crossed the bridge, perhaps because one left, with the Roundstone coast, the lee of Errisbeg, so that the full force of the prevailing wind struck here. I crossed it on a chilly evening, the sky grey but conserving its rain, the sea calm. A man was fishing with a line from the middle of the bridge, drawing, for it was Friday, his supper from the green water below.

Once on Inishnee the wind seemed to drop or was made less palpable by the humped contour of the island. Quitting the road, I began to circle the northern coast. It was easy to climb over the low stone walls that came running down to meet the rocks of the shore and divided the small fields, but the going was more difficult over the weedy rocks themselves but a few yards from the steely water.

I had come to find something marked on the Ordnance Survey map as an antiquity, but the name was smudged and indecipherable, so I did not know exactly what to look for. At what I judged to be the approximate point, I came upon a meadow, a *llon*, of dark-green grass dotted with what looked like the remains of pillars or the corners of a foundation perhaps. But they did not seem ancient; it was more likely that some persevering cultivator had made this attempt to rid his land of stony obstruction. I thought of lines from the song called 'The Rocks of Bán':

> O I wish the Queen of England
> Would write and send for me
> For I'd rather fight her battles
> Far from my own country;
> I'd rather die a soldier
> In the grey twilight of dawn
> Than stay beside you, Sweeney
> To plough the rocks of Bán.

The words belong to the nineteenth century, and, though the tune is far older, its tragic lilt may always have been attached to some expression of the heart-breaking toil by which a living is barely scraped from fields such as these.

As I followed the coastline around, two small boys and a dog tracked my movements, watching all I did but keeping their distance. From the top of an earthen hedge surrounding a steep little pasture higher than the rest where a few sheep were grazing, I scanned the scene for a trace of broken walls or standing-stones. I knew how antiquities can melt into a landscape as if they did not wish to be found, how clever they are in concealing themselves in their surroundings. As I looked south to where the island narrowed in a kind of waist, I could see an enormous rock like a tooth jutting from a desert of smaller boulders that hemmed the shore on the eastern side. Though seemingly a natural formation, it was, I surmised, a focus for local phantasy owing to its striking size and shape. But it could not be what I sought, for its situation did not agree with the blurred Irish letters on the map.

Having reached the northernmost tip of the island without finding anything, I was beginning to retrace my steps, keeping yet nearer to the sea, when suddenly there appeared two strange structures of stone, unmortared and built on the flat rock just above the high-water line. One was a pyramidal carn, about five feet in height, the other a half-circle of wall somewhat lower, screening a *bullán*, or basin, scooped out of the rock and filled with water. Between this and the wall stood a glass jar of the wild irises that grow on marshy land all about here at this season, and both structures were decorated with these yellow flags and with twigs of rhododendron, pittosporum and fuchsia stuck into the chinks between their stones.

There was no image, no hint of a dedication, but a feeling of quietude and enchantment hung over the spot. Was it Christian or pagan, well of saints or fairy-well – who knows? It was, however, surely a shrine to those powers of the place that endure, by whatever name they are known, for unnumbered ages. The flowers were beginning to fade, so perhaps the date of festival was just past; or were the withering shoots renewed each Sunday and so due for replacement in two days' time?

There are many of these *bullán* in Ireland, and whether hollowed out by natural or supernatural forces, or by 'ceremonial attrition' as some have thought, they are even today accredited with miraculous properties. Sometimes they are cups, sometimes basins; sometimes they occur singly, sometimes in groups. The one dedicated to St Cailin near Slyne Head, between Roundstone and Mannin Bay, is said to be 'on a little height within a stone, which never overflows the stone nor becomes dry'. Certainly the water in the one before me was clear and without brackish taint, exactly filling its basin to the top. I looked into its candid eye but could see no votive pin or coin sunk within.

The little boys were perhaps its custodians and followed me in anxious shyness, hoping that I, a stranger, would not see the evidence of their piety. Once I had come upon the well, they disappeared altogether. I felt that it was a secret place and that they would not like to be questioned about it, though a sincere folklorist, I have no doubt, would have tried to gather first-hand information from them. But I always shrink from examining people on their traditional beliefs, feeling as I do that only long dwelling in and upon such ambience will reveal anything of value.

But the timid children could scarcely have had a more sympathetic visitor to their shrine, and I added to its decoration a sprig of that heather with especially large magenta bells, the *Erica mediterranea* which grows around Errisbeg hill. In Cornwall I have always wished to garland the stone circles and offer flowers before crosses so ancient that they seem symbols of resurrection rather than of pain. But, alas, to deck a well there is no longer part of the century's mind, and, if it is done, it is usually no more than a propagandist revival or antiquarian eccentricity – tolerated, indeed, only because the belief that might once have inspired it has now sunk too far below the surface to influence general action.

In Ireland it is otherwise, for some direct supersensual contact still endures, deeper than anything that can be expressed at rational level and able to formulate itself in traditional observance. A ritual plunge into the cosmic dream, the holy unconscious, is here a possibility yet, though less generally accepted than it once was.

Rustic ceremony is always touching, the simplicity of the magical instruments used seeming to enhance rather than to mitigate their power. In his novel *Hidden Faces* Salvador Dalí describes a cross of unhewn branches set up in the forest where a pastoral preacher and his flock celebrated their campestral rites. And once in County Kerry I assisted at a cottage mass, a relic of the penal times. It is continued today for convenience if the nearest church is some miles distant, for a number of neighbours join together and invite the priest to celebrate in one of their homes. So the kitchen was transformed into a sanctuary, and the long table, raised on two chains and draped with the best embroidered linen, became an altar. The household candles were set in tin scones from the local hardware store, the vases were jam jars filled with flowers lately growing in hedges near by, the paten a kitchen plate, the spoon a plated teaspoon, the lavabo a china soap dish. The neighbours who had gathered kneeled on the stone floor, the women's shawls, black or brown, contrasting with the sea-green wash of the cottage walls, while the wild sea itself beat on rocks beyond the window pane. The red and yellow of the parish priest's cope had run together as though this very fabric had been soaked in salt water. During the elevation, bacon and sausages sizzled in pans on a turf fire at the end of the room, and a kettle hanging from an iron hook boiled merrily, and soon the table was back in normal use for the breakfast of the hungry worshippers.

But what of the basin on Inishnee and the strange structures beside it? Were they some fragment of stone-and-well worship? Hardiman, in his notes to *A Chorographical Description of West or H-Iar Connaught* by O'Flaherty, says:

> In the west of Iar-Connaught, they sometimes erect a pile of stones on the shore, bearing a rude resemblance to a small house or castle, which they offer to some imaginary being or goblin, and expect a fair wind in return. But this is considered a serious affair, and can never be repeated by the same individual.

Further on, a reference is made to a chapel dedicated to St Mathias on Inishnee, and 'another place in memory of St Brendan'. In his *Conamara*, Sean Mac Giollarnáth says:

> A house of the Dominican Order was founded here when O'Flaithearta held Bailenahinse, and St Breandán had followers in this neighbourhood, for his name is still connected with the island.

Somehow I do not think that what I found was St Mathias's Chapel nor anything to do with the Dominican foundation, but it may have been 'the place in memory of St Brendan'. O'Donovan, in *Ordnance Survey Letters of Co. Galway*, tells us that in the parish of Abbey Gormegan 'there is a well called Tobar Breanainn (St Brendan's Well) associated with a heap of stones where pilgrims pray', and his map actually marks another Tobar Breanainn on Inishnee. I have no doubt that the tiny shrine which I discovered is still the scene, at the appropriate date, of a turrus – that is, the performance of 'rounds' or 'stations'. The turrus marks the day of the saint to whom the well owes its virtue or that of some other festival locally celebrated. The well and other structures – altars, carns or other stones – are circumambulated sunwise a specified number of times, usually three or nine, the pilgrims sometimes crawling on hands and knees, 'Paters' and 'Aves' are recited at intervals, the well water is drunk and forehead and hands bathed in it. An offering is commonly made to the guardian spirit of the place, something metallic being thrown into the water or a shred of clothing left near by. A little of the water is often taken home by the pilgrims, losing none of its efficacy.

Though today these devotions are always performed in the name of some saint, it is significant that the Church has never formally authorized them and in some places barely tolerates them. Many 'patterns' have, indeed, been puritanically suppressed, less on account of the obvious traces of pagan survival in their rites than because of the fairs frequently held at the same time. These were naturally accompanied by dancing, drinking, courting and a certain amount of fighting, the disorder being not the least part of the enjoyment.

I cannot help wondering if the word turrus may not be cognate with the classical word *truare*, which, as W.F. Jackson Knight has shown, meant to circumambulate with magical intent. Turrus has long been adopted into English and the whole performance called turrusing.

But which of the two St Brendans is commemorated on Inishnee, he of Clonfert or he of Birr? One of them has a festival on 16 May, which would explain the fading decorations at the shrine. Though the former is St Brendan the Navigator, whose voyages were as famous as those of Maeldún and Snegdus, it was one of Brendan of Birr's disciples who was found by Maeldún and his followers on one of their remotest landfalls. Whichever Brendan it was, he seems to have called at most of the numerous islands off the coasts of Kerry and Connacht, and some that do not figure on any modern map. Surely he is the kind of imaginary being who, in return for delicate attentions, might 'grant a fair wind'.

Legendary Background

I N THE INTENSE cold of late evening the further shores of Bertraghboy Bay seemed to catch and hold the last of the sunlight, the seawrack below high-water line glowing orange, the walled fields above burnished green, the far mountains an unpaintable blue. The bay was a mirror catching sunset's reflection in the eastern sky.

Almost due south from Roundstone, hardly to be distinguished on the horizon, lay St MacDara's Isle. The saint is still venerated in these parts, but his island is deserted, and the ruins of his monastic settlement, though well preserved so far, would repay more attention. The name MacDara is common in the isles to this day.

Much nearer, only a little to the south-west of Inishnee, is the island of Inishlackan – Inish Leacainn in Irish, the Shelving Island. But the old name for it was Inish Leih Dhuine, the Island of the Grey Man, and it is the breath of this Grey Man that still broods over it at the approach of twilight, and, once darkness has fallen, it is his shadow that takes possession of the place. At night, none of the islanders will leave their houses. On some friends of mine, who spent several summers there in conditions of extreme hardship, the unbroken silence had a different effect. They found the quiet indoors so oppressive on a calm night that they felt obliged to go outside, many hours before dawn, to hear some sound at least, even were it only the wash of waves on a strand.

Their cottage was built so close to the sea that a storm or a high tide would bring water flooding under the door. A strong wind would burst the door open. The walls inside were green with damp, for no one lived there during the winter, and even in summer a turf fire continually burning was a necessity. Their only link with the mainland was a rotting boat, which they somehow learned to manage. The currents of the channel dividing Inishnee from Erraloch were treacherous, especially in bad weather, but there was no shop on the island, and even their drinking-water had to be fetched from Roundstone, as their well often ran dry. Sometimes they had lived for several days on potatoes and tea when they manoeuvred the boat into the inlet of Erraloch.

This craft had been so long beached during the winter months that the timbers were beginning to gape, and soon it became quite unseaworthy. Their only alternative was to borrow a boat from one of the islanders, but this matter could never be broached directly. They had to lead up to it by an hour-long conversation on every possible subject, their neighbour well knowing what they wanted but determined to make them pay for it by entertaining him. He would play them like fish on a line, pretending that there was some insuperable obstacle to the loan and only giving way after many jokes, anecdotes and general cajolery. Who can blame him? Opportunities for diversion were few on the island of the Grey Man. Besides, a blunt request would have been in deplorably bad taste by Inishlackan standards and therefore deserving of a snub. But these circumlocutions were exasperating to victims whose nerves were strung by hunger and the threat of an approaching gale.

One of their neighbours on the island, a young man living with his father, continually declared that he could hear the 'little people' talking at the gable-end of his house. Who or what are these little people, and why does belief in them persist throughout the Celtic countries even into this age of space travel, nuclear physics and astronomically figured finance? Beside the flat denial of the 'common-sense' sceptic, who would put it all down to insanity or drink, many serious attempts at explanation have come from different angles, whether psychological, anthropological or theological.

Some have stated that fairies are the dead and the fairy faith an attenuated form of ancestor worship. The fact that stories of these beings are often associated with prehistoric burial mounds gives colour to the theory, but it does not fully cover the facts – unless we assume that the dead are very much alive.

Another suggests that fairy traditions conserve a memory of earlier races of men – taller, like the Tuatha-de-Danaan, or shorter, like the leprechauns – than present-day humanity, or that actual remnants of such races surviving until comparatively recent times in remote localities provided a basis for legend. It is true that much that is told of fairyland in folklore accords well with what can be deduced of Bronze Age culture, and fairy 'palaces' are often located on the site of a neolithic or Bronze Age dwelling. But this explanation is again inadequate, for it does not take full account of the range in size ascribed to these beings. This varies from the gigantic to the minuscule, from those that hurl a twenty-ton rock as a plaything or need a whole mountain for a chair to the tiny guardian of hidden treasure:

> He's a span
> And a quarter in height.
> Get him in sight, hold him tight,
> And you're a made
> Man!

Ecclesiastical authorities have plainly stated that fairies are 'demons' – at best this is mitigated to 'fallen angels'. But any religion, once its ascendancy is assured, tends to relegate the pantheon of its predecessor to the nether regions. Though the Church has often discouraged preoccupation with fairies, it has never denied their existence, nor could it do so and remain consistent with its own tenets.

A fourth explanation, if such it can be called, is the one put forward in *The Brownies* by Juliana Horatia Ewing. This takes the view that fairies are children seen through the eyes of an adult, their small stature, intense phantasy life and the irresponsible mischief natural to them – which may be transformed into helpfulness – supplying a foundation for the stories. Little need be said of this, since it is in the main a sentimental moralizing of the problem and deals with but one of the many types of fairy, Milton's 'drudging goblin' or 'lubber fiend'.

More serious is the theory that fairies are the last devotees of a pre-Christian religion, the widespread but loosely organized cult of the witches. Certainly fairies share with witches the use of rustic herblore and other traditional medicine, supernormal powers like foreknowledge, thought transference and shape-shifting, the faculty of cursing and the gift of the spell. Both are 'riders to Diana', their strangely caparisoned cavalcades to be glimpsed galloping through the twilight to banquet or dance. But it would be a mistake to draw this parallel so far as to confuse identities: witches were always human, whatever secret powers they may have developed within them, while fairies are something other.

It can hardly be true that everyone who has claimed experience of the fairy clan must have been 'through other' or else confused by that last glass of potheen. The evidence is too voluminous and too well attested to be thus despised. Perhaps its most striking feature is the full documentation on the physical disappearance of those subsumed into the fairy realm, either permanently or returning after some lapse of time to recount their adventures.

One of the best-accredited of the former cases comes from among the Scottish-Irish of Aberfoyle, where the Reverend Robert Kirk, author of *The Secret Commonwealth of Elves, Fauns and Fairies*, was minister till 1692, when he 'went to his owne herde'. In Sir Walter Scott's time, the churchyard at Aberfoyle contained his tomb, but the tomb contained no remains. The story is that while wandering over the local 'fairy hill' – probably a ráth – he fell unconscious and was presumed dead. He later appeared to a relative, imploring him to tell Graham of Duchray, a mutual cousin, that he (Kirk) was not dead but imprisoned in fairyland and could only be released by Duchray's dirk thrown over his head. Kirk promised to be present at the baptism of his posthumous child, and so he was, but his cousin Duchray had not sufficient presence of mind to perform the magical operation of casting the *scéan dhu* over the apparition, so Kirk was never restored to his manse.

'A black knife bring to cross my sorrow,' as the imprisoned girl in Samuel Ferguson's poem sings, for this knife, analogous to the athame of the witches, if not identical with it, is one of the most effective weapons for rescuing a mortal from fairy thrall.

Ireland can provide many similar stories, notably what is perhaps the most striking instance of the second category of disappearances, those from which the exile returns. Morogh O'Lee was strolling one day in melancholy mood along the coastal reaches of the barony of Ballynahinch after a quarrel with his wife. He was approached by some strangers who blindfolded him and carried him off in a boat, uncovering his eyes only when they reached the island of Hy-Brasil. They spoke both Irish and English and after two days brought him back 'to the sea-Point of Galway' – possibly the region of Curardacrugh, east of Cashla Bay, is intended – where they left him. He made his way to a neighbouring cottage and there lay sick for some weeks, finally returning to Galway town.

He did not, however, return empty-handed, for he brought with him a book, which it seems he spent the next seven years in studying. Thereafter he began to practise as a doctor, though without any other training, and continued successfully in this profession till the end of his life.

His inspiration, called *The Book of Hy-Brasil*, may be seen today in the library of the Irish Academy. It is a manuscript on vellum, in Irish and Latin of the fifteenth century, and consists of forty-six large quarto folios that look like a series of astrological charts. But if the book is palpable enough, the island of its provenance is not: Hy-Brasil is one of the most famous of the 'vanishing' islands. It is not to be found on maps today, though it appears, in various latitudes, off the Connacht coast on several ancient ones, notably those of Dalerto in 1325 and of Fra Mauro in 1459. It has been sighted from the Aran Islands, westward but is said to emerge from its concealing veil only once in seven years. Similar stories are told of the coast towards St David's Head in Wales:

> Green Fairy Islands, reposing
> In sunlight and beauty on ocean's calm breast

whose strange inhabitants, as recently as last century, would visit Milford Haven and Laugharne to do their marketing.

A little further west than the spot where Morogh O'Lee was landed, the Skird Rocks and Carrickmackan in Casheen Bay become the scene of illusory landscapes, towers – sometimes on fire – crowds of people, stacks of turf and corn, ships coming and going. But these visions, though they occur on cloudy days as often as on fine, may be classed as mirages, like the famous Fata Morgana in the Straits of Messina. The rocky islets themselves are permanent and solid features of the scene, only occasionally becoming clothed with a more dramatic life. It is otherwise with Hy-Brasil, which is an island from another world, an earthly paradise, like Moy Mel – Magh Meala, the Plain of Honey, and Tir na nÓg, the Country of the Young. The name Hy-Brasil is the Island of Great Desire, and Morogh O'Lee may have spent some of his stay in 'drinking of luscious wine amidst flowers of the sun's own hue'. It was while searching for this fabled paradise that the Portuguese navigator Cabral discovered Brazil, which was named after it.

The story of Morogh O'Lee is a version of that constantly recurring myth whose theme is the imparting of wisdom to humanity through semi-divine or supernatural beings. Not only medicine, but metalwork, agriculture, music, poetry and the written character have had this origin claimed for them.

Though many strands have, at different times, contributed to the skein of the fairy tradition, the truest explanation is the most unlikely – that fairies are beings inhabiting a supersensual plane which interpenetrates the universe normally perceptible to human senses and is often particularly linked to a locality in the physical world.

If this is so, then the first hypothesis is true only in so far as the dead may be assumed to use a subtle body analogous to that of fairy beings, so that fairies, though not identical with the human dead, nevertheless inhabit the same plane of existence and therefore came to be confused with them in the popular mind.

The second explanation is almost contained in the first, for earlier races now form part of the dead. But perhaps it was about the time of the late neolithic or early Bronze Age that man began to lose his early kinship with supersensual beings, so that they tend to appear to him in the habiliments of this period.

The third theory, or rather dogma, is tendentious, since a praeter-human entity is not necessarily evil or even hostile to mankind. The fourth resembles the second, in that the child sometimes retains for a while the same openness to super-sensual life enjoyed by the primitive adult; while the fifth confuses teacher with taught, for the lore of the Wicca came from contact with other worlds.

But the bodily vanishing of those who, in the legends of Gaeldom, visit such worlds remains a puzzle; it is clearly not a case of astral projection in those many instances when the physical body disappears with the subtle. It seems rather to be a kind of dematerialization, which may be followed by a precipitation or rematerializing later on.

In a land of sunsets, this evening's was perhaps the most striking I had seen. A huge wisp of vapour was streaming up from the north-west like smoke from a monstrous bonfire – dove-grey, brown, russet, copper, gold – its tones reflected by the cloudbank above the Twelve Bens. This smoke from the giant's fire gradually thinned out, dissipating itself across the mid-heaven; the sky colours that stained the mountains – for these had taken on the same hues as the cumulus, were clouds that had gained substance – changed from copper to rose, massive against unclouded stretches of a subdued but translucent blue. One may forgive the sceptic who declares that to such sunsets and their stimulation of the phantasy Hy-Brasil owes its origin.

Finvarra and the
Seven Daughters

I WISH THAT on our drive westward we had been able to make a detour to the north in the direction of Tuam, between Ballinasloe and Athenry, if only because of this district's association with Finvarra of Knockmaa, fairy chieftain of Connacht. Here for centuries he held sway – no diminutive sprite but a being on the heroic scale, demigod rather than elf, riding a black charger with fiery nostrils. Young girls of the west used to dance all night with Finvarra in their dreams, and perhaps even today he has not been entirely ousted by the image of Gregory Peck, Marlon Brando or whoever the current favourite of the screen may be. As a focus for the phantasy life, is there much to choose?

Writing in 1839, O'Donovan says that Finvarra was a particular friend of John Kirwan (who repaired his cashels for him) and of Mrs Kirwan, who, about ten years previously, erected for him 'two chimerical cyclopean buildings'. The matter-of-fact style of this note seems not only to take for granted the existence of the fairy chief but to accept him as the friend of a well-known family with no more comment than if he were a retired colonel living in the neighbourhood. Finvarra himself appears mundane enough to take an interest in repairs to masonry and building projects, and, had I been in the area, I would certainly have searched for those cashels and cyclopean structures. The latter would, I suppose, in England come into the category of follies, but surely no others have had so strange an origin. I hope that both they and the repaired cashels – which were probably neolithic forts – still exist; they may do so, for this record of the supernatural friendship of the Kirwans dates back only a hundred years or so, and, for all I know, there may be references to it still more recent.

There is a St Barry, whose name bears a suspicious likeness to that of the fairy king, and one wonders whether he may not, in common with many Cornish saints, whose histories are unknown to all but the most fanciful hagiologists, be a pagan demigod in thin disguise. Certainly Finvarra, when described as a tall man dressed in black, and his wife as a beautiful lady with a silver veil, are not unknown to another tradition.

Lady Wilde says that one of the Kirwans of Castle Hackett was given a bride and many presents of gold and jewels in return for aiding the chief on one of his forays against a rival fairy faction. She also recounts how another member of the family won an important race through the loan, by the helpful Finvarra, of a jockey from among his own people. But she mentions no dates, so one cannot tell whether these events took place before or after the repairing of the cashels by John Kirwan. In any case, the family was apparently on easy terms with the fairy chief for generations. Finvarra himself does not seem to have been entirely faithful to his queen, Onagh, but to have had an inclination for mortal women if they were sufficiently good-looking. He is very fully characterized in legend – or might one not say in history? – unlike the mysterious Grey Man, who gave his name to Inishlackan but remains the shadow of shade. Who or what was he, divinity or mortal long dead? And who were the Seven Daughters after whom many sacred wells in the region were named? Study of maps reveals that the nymph of the well, who showed herself otherwhere to devotees as a supernatural salmon or trout, like Connla's Salmon of Wisdom, here kept her human shape but multiplied herself sevenfold or subdivided herself into as many aspects, her influence in this guise still haunting the Connacht springs.

One of these wells is to be found near Ross in the town-land of Munterowen – perhaps the one which O'Flaherty mentions as situated on the west side of the Hill of Doon – 'a well in memory of the seven daughters'. There is another one in the Maamturk range, yet another on the opposite side of the haven to Roundstone, away towards Carna, and a third on Aranmore.

Further to the north-west, at Renvyle, south of Blacksod Bay, there is a holy well in the ruined church belonging to the castle, which keeps their memory fresh. This church, like many another, may have been built on a pagan sanctuary. In former times there was also a Stone of the Seven Daughters, which would bring a blight on one's enemies if turned widdershins while an imprecation was uttered. There are many of these stones scattered throughout the west, and they are not without benefi-cent uses, in healing and fertility, if turned deosil. But works of malediction and death are easier to perform, human nature being what it is, so they are usually known as cursing stones. O'Flaherty says that this stone was 'taken away and buried by the parish priest, at which the people were much dissatisfied'.

Who were these Sacred Seven? One tradition – probably a late one – says that they were saints, another the daughters of a British king, yet another those of a king of Leinster. But these are historical rationalizations or mere moralizing, as in the case of the Well of the Holy Women near Teelin, County Donegal, who are supposed to be three sisters: Sense, Understanding and Modesty. The date of their festival, however, 23 June, is so near the summer solstice as to make one suspect a more ancient lineage, foreign to these sedate allegories. Fishermen used to salute this spring as they passed along the shore near it by lowering their sails and raising their caps. Thus do Moslem sailors, even today, when, following the south-eastern coast of Cyprus, they sight the Tekke of Umm Harâm. This mosque was built over the tomb of the Prophet's aunt, who, on this very spot, fell off her mule and 'broke her pellucid neck', as the *Excerpta Cypria* says. The actual tomb is a trilithon, which long antedates the era of Islam, so here again the relic is far more ancient than the observations that seek to explain it. The huge structure is draped with dark-green velvet, and the slant-eyed sheik, suspicious of the infidel's curiosity, hurries one around muttering prayers under his breath. He would not consider it tactful if one prodded the hangings to discover whether, as some of the faithful still aver, the lintel stone does not rest on the two supporting columns but hangs miraculously suspended between heaven and earth.

I like to think that another Donegal well may have had a Seven Daughters dedication, though I do not know whether this is so. I found it long ago as I wandered along the winding shores a little way north of Burtonport on a day when the air imparted a translucent greyness to all it touched. The unrippled sea lay in whorls of a greenish grey, the banked-up dunes with their hem of rock and strand rounded the coast in horizontal loops of a buffish grey, while spanning clouds rose from a far but distinct skyline in arches of an oyster grey to the nacreous zenith. So little colour tinged the air that one could not tell whether the strips and lagoons to the west were true sky or yet more distant cloud.

Nothing moved; everything shimmered faintly in the subdued daylight. The cries of gulls around the humpback islands, skirted with tawny seaweed, the voices of boys by the sea's edge, screaming in Irish as they swarmed over the rocks, and the yelps of their collie darted with so keen a quality through the stillness that they seemed unreal.

The tide was ebbing as if mesmerized. The boys dipped out of sight behind a curve of one of the islands, one that still showed traces of a castle's rampart. Their calling ceased, and another sound became perceptible.

Around the furthest stony peninsula visible to the north-west, where stood a church in ruins all but the tower, a promontory covered with smoothly cropped grass was joined to the mainland by a concrete breakwater scarcely a foot wide. The top of this miniature isthmus was almost awash, the water on either side being a full seven feet deep. To the right, it was sluggish and clotted with foam, writhing in oriental patterns over its surface; to the left, it swayed back and forth foamlessly, caressing stone and concrete with a delicate shock.

Above this divided channel, but sunk in the close grass of the mainland and sheltered by the dunes, a tiny square well, incredibly clear, mirrored the sky and its own steep sides. It was so near the sea that it must, one would have thought, be tainted with salt. But its water was as fresh in taste as in colour.

Here from inland there floated a sound of music, fitful at first but gaining in confidence. It seemed to trouble the surface of the well with a shiver, though too distant for distinguishable tune. As the melody grew gradually more articulate, it seemed so old as to be both comforting and frightening. The pipes were neither martial nor eerie in tone, neither sorrowful nor gay, but perennial. They moaned, mused and twittered, rising and falling like the waves of the tide, the notes turning back on themselves or mounting, self-borne, to die away in a spiral – running evenly, halting or twisting. One air melted into another without pause, chant-like; the tunes were played seemingly without passion or comprehension and asked nothing of their listener; simply, they had being.

The piper was a peg-legged man sitting on a low wall outside a cabin, one of several small houses surrounded by patches of cultivation just inland from the dunes. While he played, a half-circle of girls in faded cottons stood listening, their mop-heads bent as if spellbound by the third string of the Dagda's harp. This lame musician was perhaps one of

Ireland's last pipers, for there cannot be many left now, apart from those who seek to revive the traditional art.

The heart-rending lilt of genuine Gaelic airs calls to something more archaic than the musical ear, something deeper than taste or reason. These snatches of melody seize, often by the simplest means, an inexpressible mood, a noetic vision of the country's soul that words can never convey. English words, at least – perhaps a born Gaelic speaker might gain from the language and give by the same means a glimpse of that vivid, poignant, unreclaimed world that hovers on the horizon, broods above lake water, lurks in the shade of an isolated thorn, cries in the wind. Small wonder that the 'Coulin' and other traditional tunes are said to have been not composed but recorded by mortals who overheard the music of the secret kingdom.

Another healing well is called the Basin of the Four Beautiful Ones, near which is their stone 'bed', wherein, should a pilgrim sleep, all his ailments would be relieved. There are many instances of the wonder-working 'saint's bed' – but were they saints, the Four Beautiful Ones? Were they even human? The lore concerning them has now grown so hazy that one cannot tell whether their beauty was moral or physical nor even whether it was male or female.

In Cornwall I have never found an ancient well grown sour and choked with water-weed without feeling an impulse to clean it out; each well should have its guardian who would see to this from time to time. But in Ireland such cleaning was considered a hazardous duty, for, though it might produce fine weather for the seafarer (by a kind of sympathetic magic, the clear water to reflect a clear sky), some member of the industrious one's family might die on account of it.

The theme of the well and its presiding spirit in these scraps of legend may not only be compared with stories from other lands but supplemented by one's own dreams or intuitions. Once I had a dream of three nymph-like figures dressed in green who stood under an apple tree, the ground at their feet made marshy by the welling-up of spring waters that would cure every ill. A luck-bearing dream, bringer of reassurance. Surely these beings were not Sense, Understanding and Modesty but a manifestation of the Triple Goddess herself, traces of whom still linger in much well worship. But the Seven Daughters, now hardly more than a name, belong to a different symbolism, sidereal rather than lunar and older than the cult of sun or moon.

Midsummer

O N THE DAY before the Corpus Christi procession was due to pass through the village, people were white- or colour-washing their houses, arranging holy pictures and statuettes in the windows and fastening sprigs of flowering shrub to the gates. Next day was so wet that the procession was put off till the following Sunday, but, though it proved fine and windless, no procession wound along the street, and the day after the flower decorations had been thrown out.

The house was full, so I had to move into the stable where there was a room opening on the yard. This I preferred to the room I had in the house because it was quieter; and then in the yard-room I had my own turf fire, which I could light at any time and feed from the stacks in the sheds outside.

I had planned to pack my cases in the morning, paving them beautifully as a first layer with the harder objects and gradually fitting things in like a mosaic. But it was a fine day, so the other visitors swept my possessions into rugs and carried them into the stable-room. This had yet to be made ready, so some things were left behind, being dumped loose on the landing. We then went off to bathe at Gorteen Strand on the other side of Roundstone village.

Here, towards one of the white beaches, sloped a cemetery where the Celtic crosses, dark against the windy sky, reminded me of the graveyard in Julien Gracq's *Au Château d'Argol* and of Albert scratching the name of the fateful woman he has not yet seen on an uninscribed cross. In lands like this and parts of

Brittany, where the soil has little depth, advantage is often taken of the seashore dunes for interment.

Here the sea was literally aquamarine in colour, but ice cold in spite of the sun. Only in one other place – the Scilly Islands – have I found water of such a Mediterranean blue and of such an arctic temperature. In both places I have bathed when the water was so cold that it was almost hot, stinging the flesh as one swam through it.

In the afternoon we set off through Ballynahinch to Lough Inagh which lay, a glistening expanse, in the long empty valley between the inland slopes of the Twelve Pins and the seaward face of the Maamturk range. This region is scarcely inhabited, its vastness and desolation seeming Scottish rather than Irish. It has the air of being almost unvisited; and of its scattered dwellings, even, some are deserted. There were a few cattle browsing near the lake's edge and a boat with fishermen silhouetted on the water towards the further shore; otherwise no sign of life.

Sunlight was casting enormous shadows from clouds driven by a wind almost too strong for us to light our spirit-stove. The turf underfoot was like a full sponge; I took off my shoes to walk on it, for this bog water, though good for the feet, will seep through and spoil any leather. The sensation was so pleasant that I thought again how much one misses of sensual variety by the constant wearing of shoes. They make the feet at once dull and soft, and in these regions, when roads were few or none, no one thought of travelling the bogs anything but barefoot. Children today are still to be seen shoeless and sometimes tinkers, but the smugness of conventional comfort is fast catching up on even the wildest Connachtman.

Looking across the lake to the 'back' of the Twelve Pins, Ben Corr and Ben Collaghduff, I made some ink sketches of the mountains. They sweep up, completely bare, from the lake fringe to the clouds, small trees and shrubby islets at their base. On the way back we stopped under Derryclare so that I could draw the striking ridge of quartz that juts from its northern flank. A burst of sunlight after rain will make the mica on all these bald crowns glint through their sparse mosses.

Such hills should interest rock climbers, yet few seem to explore them. There are no cafés or climbing huts, still less notices to indicate a fine view; nothing but 'wildness and wet'. Some antiquities are marked on the Ordnance Survey map, but one must find one's own way to them. Legend tells how St Patrick came eastward after his triumph on the holy mountain to bless Connemara from these heights, and his stone 'bed' and well are still to be found in the Maamturk range.

Back at Roundstone in the late evening I caught sight of a fire on the lower slopes of Cashel Mountain across Bertraghboy Bay, then another on the outskirts of Roundstone itself, then one towards Toombeola, the smoke drifting heavily on the quiet air. I recognized the sun fires of St John's Eve, still spontaneously lit by the people, a custom kept without interruption from prehistoric ages – not revived, as in Cornwall, by antiquarian societies. Here they explain or, rather, attempt to Christianize the practice by telling (with indifference to the gospel narrative) that St John the Baptist suffered martyrdom by burning, and a bone is flung into the flames to represent the saint's body. Afterwards, when the fire is cooling, a little of the ash is saved by the head of each household and kept to ward off evil in the coming year.

Traditionally, a bonfire should be lit in each town-land, a land division going back to the Gelfine system of tenure based on the ancient Brehon laws. Several groups of people, usually blood relations, hold adjacent tracts of land, each constituting a 'quarter' of the town-land. It is a compromise between common holding and private ownership and is useful, as much agricultural work can be done more easily and pleasantly with the help of neighbours.

The day marked the summer solstice, and it was not

difficult to divine the pagan substratum below the Christian overlay in these fire rites and watch the taming of an ancient ceremony of sun worship. (But what a Midsummer! Windless now but grey and cold in the evening.)

Soon a ring of bonfires sprang up, a new one being lit elsewhere as one died down. I counted twelve blazing at once – on Inishnee and the coast behind it by Glinisk and beyond again towards Carna in the Gaeltacht and the island of Mweenish. It is said that the more you can count at one time the better, as each represents a year of good luck in the future; this is one of many auguries to be drawn from the Midsummer fires, two of which were blazing on the Roundstone jetties. Their aromatic scent made me wonder, remembering the nine herbs thrown on the Cornish beacons, whether anything were added to the sticks and turf.

I went near to the bonfire lit beyond the bridge leading to Inishnee, drawn by the blaze through the grey air. A small group of boys was tending it, while younger children played near and three donkeys were trotting about, a little girl dressed in red riding one of them. This was, I supposed, the last remnant of that driving of farm beasts and children through the embers to keep them from harm, the suffumigation that guaranteed them a year's health.

Why should the name of the Baptist be linked to a fire festival? It would seem more appropriate if he patronized a healing well, blessed a fishery or presided over some aquatic rite, as indeed he does in some parts of Europe. But water cults are often interchanged with fire cults, and the St John here celebrated is less a historical personage than a name attached to an elemental power, one of André Breton's *grandes transparentes* – presences known by inference, who have lurked in Europe's unconscious for countless ages, taking on names, now pagan, now Christian, as times changed. St John manifests in a fire symbolizing the sun in splendour, St Michael is chthonic, St George of protean nature, a wanderer, loved by the gypsies.

There may be another reason for associating the Baptist with the sun. Is not the severed head a dominant theme in Celtic myth, as instance the stories of Sualtam and of Bran? And has it not appeared in Yeats's later plays, *A Full Moon in March* and *The King of the Great Clock-Tower*? Though the author was perhaps more directly influenced by Wilde's Iokannan than by Celtic legend, he says in his preface: 'it is part of the old ritual of the year: the mother goddess and the slain god'. The image of the clock tower is significant in regard to man's measurement of time by the great luminaries.

Frazer relates a story of a hunter for golden fern seed who shoots at the sun, from which fall three fertilizing drops of blood. St John is perhaps the Midsummer sun when, the solstice reached, his power begins to decline or, rather, sun and bleeding head are both symbols of the power that impregnates moon and earth.

One thinks, too, of those ancient Irish prophecies of the visitation called variously the Rowing Wheel, the Fiery Bolt and the Broom out of Fanaid, which shall fall on the land one St John's Day. The Feast of the Decollation of St John seems to be referred to, rather than Midsummer Day, but here again the severed head is linked with wheel and fire. The effects of this vengeance resemble those of a hydrogen bomb. Here is St Moling's account of it:

> In John's festival will come an assault
> Which will traverse Erinn from the south-west
> A furious dragon which will burn all before it,
> Without communion, without sacrament.
>
> As a black dark troop will they burst in flames,
> They will die like verbal sounds;
> One alone out of hundreds
> Of them all shall but survive.

When I returned in the dusk to the yard-room, a turf fire was burning in the stone recess, and by candlelight I found the historic chamber pot repaired with a pot-mender that used to accompany boat trips from Roundstone to the Aran Islands. A party of thirty people or so would set out for the whole day and use it in turn, throwing decency to the winds. I fell asleep in the glow of the turf, as I watched the flickering flame light on the whitewashed walls.

The Martins

O N A FINE morning, E. having given me a lift as far as
the village, I walked on to Erraloch, taking my lunch
with me. I had hoped for a bathe, but, though it did
not rain, the sky became gradually veiled in that haze from the
back of the Twelve Bens which I had learned to distrust. A
chilly wind whipped the sea, so I gave up all idea of a swim.
Indeed, having found a sheltered cranny in the rocks, I did
nothing except gaze about me and read a little.

Suddenly, one of the many too-affectionate collies of the
neighbourhood sprang down beside me and refused to go. He
vanished only after I had approached his master, a man living
in a little house on the rocky shore, where a stream issued into
the sea.

'The dog won't leave me,' I said.

'You're not the first one,' he replied. 'They'll follow anyone
who'll give them a pat. He's just been beaten for the same thing.
That's why he's run off into the gardens.'

He spoke with a pleasant lilt which many people would have
called (incorrectly) a brogue. In spite of the *Oxford Dictionary*'s
suggestion, this word has nothing to do with a shoe but derives
from *biróg*, a spasm or muscular contraction in the Munster
dialect. It is the same image as in the phrase tongue-twister or
jaw-breaker and means much more than an accent or intonation;
it can only apply to one speaking a foreign language with diffi-
culty. He pointed towards some fields between unmortared
walls where the dog had disappeared. In the wilder parts of
Ireland anything that is not a mountain tends to be called a

garden, for a garden is almost any enclosure, even if there is no attempt at cultivation – a small meadow, perhaps, with some yellow flags or aubretia plants run wild and straggling fuchsia bushes. A mountain, on the other hand, need not have height – any rugged slope of heathland is a mountain.

The people do not train their dogs well; they give them no attention at home, so the creatures become a nuisance, begging for food, petting and exercise. They are sometimes mangy – cats, too, and nothing is done for them. Donkeys are left out in bad weather and go unshod, their hoofs prolonged into enormous dual toenails that crack and scale and almost trip them up. They might be the talons of a devil in a painting by Bruegel or Hieronymus Bosch. A veterinary surgeon may be too distant or too expensive, but one would think that almost anybody with a sharp knife could pare them in the early stages. If owners do not exert themselves to tend their beasts, they have no scruple about disposing of them when unwanted and often drown full-grown dogs and cats. Yet, in a small place like Roundstone, dogs lie undisturbed in the middle of the road, considerately skirted by the infrequent traffic.

The people are considered by the English to be cruel to animals, and certainly the sensitive of any nationality should avoid market day in a country town, which will scarcely pass without distressing sights. In country slaughterhouses the humane killer and the white coat may not be used unless an inspector's visit is due. Deliberate sadism is perhaps rare, but callousness leads to unnecessary violence in the handling of livestock, and where cruelty is financially profitable it will continue, as shown by the recent scandals in connection with the shipping of horses to the Continent. Domestic animals are treated rough rather than petted, sticks and stones being their reward for any misdemeanour.

Protestants blame the Catholic Church for this attitude, saying that it follows from an ecclesiastical denial of animals' rights. But some of the saints took the trouble to preach to fish and birds, to say nothing of donkeys, and a few years ago a well-known Irish newspaper carried a daily announcement that a certain cardinal had declared cruelty to animals a mortal sin. In countries where Eastern Orthodoxy prevails, beasts are at least equally unregarded.

No one has any cause for smugness on this score, for it was not until 1822 that the law afforded animals any protection in Britain. Before this date they were man's absolute property, to dispose of as he chose. And it was an Anglo-Irishman, 'Humanity' Martin, who forced the measure through as a Private Member's Bill, against the fiercest opposition from both Houses.

Richard Martin was a Martin of Ballynahinch Castle, some six miles from here, and for fifty years he represented Galway in Parliament. Not only the staunchest fighter in the defence of animals – he was a founder of the RSPCA – he was also one of the most famous duellists of his time. On one occasion, when asked who would win the election he was contesting, he replied, 'The survivor', hence his other nickname of 'Hair-Trigger Dick'. Taxed in a debate with the inconsistency implied by his two nicknames, he answered, 'An ox cannot hold a pistol, sir.' He was the Colonel Martin of Yeats's ballad with the sardonic refrain 'The Colonel went out sailing'.

His granddaughter figured in Maria Edgeworth's *Tour in Connemara*, which described a journey undertaken in 1833 when the author was sixty-six years old. She came from 'Edgeworth's Town', as she spelled it, in County Longford – the house is now converted into a convent. The discomforts and goodwill of the hospitality at Ballynahinch Castle which she described can still be paralleled in Ireland today.

When Mary Martin inherited the huge estates of Ballynahinch, said to comprise three hundred miles of coastline, she was called the Princess of Connemara. According to Miss Edgeworth, she had 'hair which might be called red by rivals

The Twelve Bens from Kylemore, Connemara

Roundstone Harbour

and auburn by lovers', the clear skin that only the Irish climate seems to produce and large blue-grey eyes. Miss Edgeworth did not think Mary precisely beautiful but said she would 'make a bust' – as we might say, she was paintable. She also had 'a good conceit of herself', a quality traditional with all the Martins, whether of Ballynahinch or of Ross. Being one of the Twelve Tribes of Galway, 'planted' during the thirteenth century, they thought there was no one to equal them anywhere. Miss Edgeworth remarked how much improved were the young girl's manners after a season in London where, though her looks were admired, her wildness and haughtiness were adversely noticed also. She herself much regretted having to modify her 'Bedouin ways'.

In spite of the remoteness of her home she had a number of suitors who visited her undaunted by the hardships of the journey, at that time considerable. It was to Roundstone that one of them, a certain Count Verdinski, retired for a few days to recover from an ineffectual attempt at suicide following a snub from Miss Mary.

The *House of Usher* atmosphere, exhaled perhaps by the haunted pool in the demesne, was perceptible in Ross even from the main road across the lake, and the intellectual distinction of Ballynahinch's heiress – linguist, philosopher and mathematician immured in her Connemara fastness – reminds one of an Edgar Alan Poe heroine. Though Mary was as healthy as the Lady Madeline was sick, she appealed to Maria Edgeworth as a model for the heroine of a Gothic novel. In fact, the poor girl was fated to be the last of her line; her forebears had left her the estate heavily in debt, due as much to philanthropy as to extravagant living for, unlike some of the other 'Tribes', they were good landlords. The only hope of retrieving her fortunes would have been a wealthy alliance, but this she was too unworldly to contract. She finally married her land agent and died poverty-stricken soon after arriving in New York, her child stillborn during the voyage.

Ross continued to be held by the other branch of the Martin family until well into the next century. When it had first been divided from Ballynahinch, one brother taking each estate, both could boast possession of an avenue twenty-one miles long, the distance between their two houses. At one time it was the largest estate in fee simple in the Three Kingdoms.

In looks, the Martins of Ross tended to be very different from their cousins of Ballynahinch, for the russet colouring grew dusky, accompanied by Spanishy eyes and an aquiline nose. Some have even said that the very name derives from the Spanish Martin or Martinez, though there seems to be little evidence to support this.

The Martins of Ross were afflicted with bad eyesight: Grandmama Martin – the one who used to say 'We all *like* men but no sensible woman could *respect* them' – one day mislaid her muff; fumbling around the drawing-room for it, she snatched the wig off the head of an old lady, one of her guests. And the ghostly fingers of an ancestress, who was almost blind, were said to investigate strangers sleeping their first night in the house. Some troops quartered there during 'the troubles' were subjected to this test and left in a hurry the next day.

Her son Robert, author of 'Ballyhooley', 'Enniscorthy' and many similar songs, next inherited Ross, and her daughter, Aunt Violet, was the Martin Ross half of the Somerville and Ross collaboration that produced *The Experiences of an Irish RM* and other works. These record a vivid picture of the Anglo-Irish society of their period, and, owing to the popularity they once enjoyed, their pellucid narrative style has perhaps been underestimated. This style was largely Violet Martin's contribution; Edith Somerville was the collector of material. But the style remained unaltered, even after Aunt Violet's death, owing, as Miss Somerville averred, to her continued contact with her partner. Having written a rough draft she would say, 'There, Violet, what do you think of that?'

and the reply would come in the rewriting of the passage with the authentic Martin touch.

The humour of their sketches and stories, as, for instance, 'Anstey's Colt', often has a sadistic slant, and the suppressed world of Gaeldom scarcely ever rises to the surface. But it does so most memorably in 'The Blood-Healer', where the life of a valuable hunter, injured in a fall, is saved by the powers of a blind fiddler met by chance on a lonely road.

Violet Martin's niece, Barbara Zavara, was the last of the line to inherit Ross, and she finally sold it during the disturbed twenties to the Land Commission. Perhaps her childhood and youth in this isolated place, before the days of cars and telephones and with few companions beside her ponies, differed little from that of Miss Mary nearly a hundred years before.

It was interesting to visit what was once Mary's home and the scene of Miss Edgeworth's stay; E. drove B.Z. and me there one afternoon. The house had long been transformed into a hotel, a destiny prefigured years ago when an extra storey was added during the ownership of the Berridge family, and it was said that this made it look like a railway hotel. It stood close under those Twelve Bens, which Miss Edgeworth referred to as the 'Seven Pins of Benabola', Ben Lettery rising dramatically above it in a tall pyramid. On this summit there used to be a *bullán* that made the hair hoar if the head was dipped in it. An imposing salmon river rushed through the demesne, emptying Ballynahinch Lough into a creek of Bertraghboy Bay, where a well dedicated to St Fechin used to stand at the junction of lake and river. Visitors were using the fishing huts, each surrounded by clumps of rhododendron, which Ranjitsinhji built on the river islands when he owned the place.

I wandered along some of the walks through woodlands of beech and conifer, eventually reaching the boathouse on Ballynahinch Lough. The air was warm and midge-haunted; no one was about, so I stripped off my clothes and plunged naked into the dark water. It was far less cold than the sea, and how much better any water feels when it envelopes the bare skin unimpeded!

At the other end of the lough, on an islet built from the stones of Toombeola Abbey, stood the original Ballynahinch Castle, now only a square tower. For ages this was a stronghold of the O'Flahertys, whose pedigree was said not to be 'stained by any but noble murders and aristocratic robberies' but who were so much feared that the Church of Ireland added a clause to its Litany, 'From the fury of the O'Flahertys, Good Lord, deliver us!' They were not, however, the first lords of Ballynahinch, being proceeded by the Mackannols, the O'Farrells and the O'Kellys and were themselves massacred by Governor Bingham. After the Restoration the Martins took over their land.

Even at the time of 'Hair-Trigger Dick', this mouldering keep was known as Mr Martin's Gaol, for it had long been used by the family as a prison. Not only did they own the land but they were also the sole magistrates in the neighbourhood, which they ruled in something not far removed from absolute monarchy.

The Barony of Ballynahinch was once co-extensive with Connemara, the name of which, says Hardiman, was once thought to be Conmaicnemara, the Bays of the Sea, but he prefers simply Conmaicne of the Sea, which distinguishes it from other districts of Connacht, all deriving from Conmac, the son of Fergus of Ulster and Queen Maeve.

Cashel and Toombeola

EVER SINCE I had been staying at Letterdyfe, I had been looking across the bay to Cashel Mountain; its dome was not lofty but singular because set apart eastward of the Twelve Bens and swelling from bogland all around. Not only was its outline less rugged that that of its neighbours but its colour was different; the skull and bones were, no doubt as theirs, of the quartzite that when weathered looks blue in the distance, but it was here covered with a coat of vegetation, olive green to the summit.

M. and I decided to walk over to it and have a look at the fort, or cashel, that gave the district its name. It was another day of mist; but one always hoped it would clear later and sometimes it did. We were offered a lift by L. and N. in their car, as far as Cashel village, which lay straggling along the foot of the mountain on one of the creeks at the head of Bertragh-boy Bay.

We made our way up the curving mountain road, no doubt a very ancient track, which led past an isolated farmstead. We were looking all the time for the cashel and eventually found it on a southern spur after the boreen had petered out. This fort was no longer well preserved, though the broken, grass-grown ramparts could still be traced, water standing in pools between every clump of rushes. Once it must have been a place of some importance with a commanding position that covered not only the seaward approaches but those inland from the east – a fortified dwelling with perhaps its attendant hamlet. On a good day the view below would have been impressive, but for us it was too misty to see far.

We scrambled down again and had a drink at the hotel, which was 'in a state of chasis' because alterations were proceeding – a little late, it is true, for the summer season, especially the fishing, had already begun; but this was Ireland. New loose covers were being fitted in the lounge and carpets laid; watercolours and drawings by contemporary Irish artists already hung on the walls.

Not far from the entrance, on the opposite side of the road, a turning led to Carna in the Gaeltacht of Galway. For cultural purposes, Ireland is divided into regions according to how much native Irish is spoken in each, those where the language still predominates being designated Gaeltacht. It was only last century, with the spread of primary education in English, that Irish was displaced as the vernacular and survived chiefly in certain districts of the western seaboard, in Cork, Kerry, Donegal and this one in Galway. Outside these areas with – most important – their accompanying islands, Irish is little spoken and, in spite of official fostering, seems, alas, to be still on the wane.

State aid may not have been an unmixed blessing – in cultural matters it seldom is – though in the circumstances it was all that could be done to save a remnant from disappearance. But the highly inflected and intricate grammar has necessarily been simplified, and the local variations, particularly of pronunciation, in Connacht, Munster and Ulster have been ironed out. The Munster dialect has been taken generally as the standard, but the result of all this has been some loss of colour, subtlety and flexibility. Children from whose homes the language has gone and who have learned it at school, as all now must, tend to enunciate with a muted or mincing timbre – to speak without *blás*. (This word means primarily taste, flavour, tang – the metaphor being transferred from food to speech.) 'You must speak it with a shiver,' as an old henwife from County Kerry once told me.

Chiefly owing to its lucky escape from Roman occupation, Ireland is the only self-governing state that has retained, from those early times, its own language. Partly from the same cause Wales also has kept its language but is not a sovereign state.

> Their tongue shall they keep
> Their land shall they lose
> Except wild Walia.

Over Brittany, as over other Celtic countries until liberated, hangs a sense of oppression, as of an alien culture imposed. Breton is still spoken, but the language is hushed when French people approach, for too often they refer to it contemptuously as a patois. But the Celtic atmosphere still envelopes the land as though it were Merlin in his cave of glass; silver light bathes the winding pathway, the hazel coppice, the stone shaggy with lichen. *Suaimhneas*, here, too; how can anyone fail to sense it and, having sensed, to treasure it?

The Celtic substratum in Britain, and to a lesser extent in France, is the collective equivalent of the repressed unconscious in the individual. It is the dream-life, the irrational, the life of phantasy and humour, and a foreigner who seeks to understand the British character should bear this in mind. It explains why the Anglo-Saxon strain, which plays the role of superego or of the Yang element, distrusts and despises the Celtic strain, the incalculable id or the Yin, making it the butt of endless jokes. Yet at the same time, almost every 'Englishman' will lay claim to Celtic blood – a grandmother from Ireland, Scottish cousins or a Welsh strain 'very far back'.

History has not worked out in favour of Celtic life patterns;

political and economic oppression and, more subtly, religious pressures have done their worst. When at last in Ireland the two former were lifted, it was already late for reinstating the ancient culture. Fragments of it survive; more fragments have been retrieved to exist, one fears, only as museum pieces for the future.

At the present day, a fourth factor must be reckoned with: science, 'progress', the pursuit of modern comfort as an end in itself and Americanization generally. What withstood coercion may well go down before artificially stimulated needs and snobbisms. Language, legend, music, dress, ways of making tools and of building, all belong together; if one goes, it means that the life pattern is broken, and the rest will follow.

The mist had thickened considerably, and a light rain was blowing in from the direction of the sea. The tide was out, leaving the estuary almost empty, but at high tide a bathe would have been possible from the jetty. We ate our lunch in a shitty cowshed above the harbour, then started to walk back to Toombeola bridge by the road that follows the edge of the sinuous creeks.

We soon picked up a lift, and I was glad of this not only on account of the rain; I had noticed, as we came along in the morning, that on the two or three miles before the bridge young horses were straying across the unfenced grazing-land beside the road. I am terrified of the quietest pony, unless it is in harness or divided from me by some substantial barrier, and these horses are seldom quiet. They will follow a stranger out of curiosity, then suddenly wheel around, kicking and plunging – 'in play', as one is always told, but what more could they do to alarm one if they were serious?

Once, when I was driving in a pony-cart from Rossbeigh to Lough Caragh in Kerry – a much pleasanter method of conveyance than a car, as long as the weather is good – we were followed by several of these unbroken colts. They galloped alongside or tore furiously around us, flinging up their heels, and I was thankful not to be on foot. Even in the pony-cart I was glad when we shook them off and entered the druid grove of Lickeen. A strange blue light filtered between those syca-mores, striking their pale stems and lying across the massed boulders below that marked a hidden rill. What is this light that, on a sudden, slants through the air of Celtic countries? Is it some effect of the combined dampness and clearness of the atmosphere – or is it something more? Leaves shiver all at once with an unheard breath, turning their undersides to catch a silvery gleam; the shadow under a tree coagulates to such an intense richness that it seems full of colour, the mouth of the 'multitudinous abyss'. Everything reflects more light and absorbs more shade than in other places.

By their long legs and flowing tails, many of the ponies here must have a dash of Arab in them. But the characteristic breed is the Connemara pony, a small, strong creature, dun-coloured with black points and a peculiar carriage of the tail. Carna used to be the centre for showing them, but now it is Clifden.

The car stopped when we reached Toombeola bridge, as the driver had some business with Mother Clancy, who was sitting on the wall outside her house with her little granddaughter. We were introduced and promised to come back later, as we wanted to look at the ruins of Toombeola Abbey before the day grew too wet. We crossed the bridge over the Owenmore River that empties Ballynahinch Lough into the sea and followed the path along the opposite side of the creek.

An overgrown graveyard lay beside this inlet of the sea, shoulder-deep in grass and fern. A roofless oratory was all that was left of the monastic buildings, a Dominican house founded by the O'Flahertys of Ballynahinch close by. An Augustinian friary, also founded by them here, had vanished completely. Rank-growing bracken choked the interior of the chapel, and a holly bush, bent over by the wind, sprouted from the eastern gable. In the south wall were two lancet-windows and a doorway with a pointed arch, to the east an empty niche; each gable-end showed where the rafters had lodged. Though all seemed utterly neglected, the cemetery was still in use, for we saw that a new grave had been dug and were told that there was to be a funeral the next day. The people cling to their ancient right of burial in a monastic precinct, though the community may long have disappeared and the convent buildings have fallen into disuse or even, as at Kilflannan, disappeared.

We returned for a much-needed whiskey to Mother Clancy's little bar. It would be difficult to be a teetotaller in Ireland, though I believe such exist; the climate makes one feel the need of a warming drink and, considering the effects, both physical and emotional, of the damp and cold, I am surprised not that there are a number of heavy drinkers but that drunkenness is not more prevalent.

Mother Clancy, her blue eyes full of gaiety and imagination, was still good-looking though her dark hair was greying and straying. She was well known in the neighbourhood for her store of tales and told us of a tradition that a chalice was buried below the niche in the chapel we had just seen or further on – she was a little vague about the situation. This reminded me of a legend telling how the Holy Grail is buried 'under a veil of lace' – the stalagmites of some Mendip cave. She also spoke of the grave of a ten-foot giant, whom she called Ben Bola as if Ben were his first name, but she must have meant the Firbolg chieftain who lies under the Twelve Bens, the Beanna Beola, and gives his name to Toombeola, too. There was an ogham stone, she said, which 'a writer' had taken away – perhaps for a museum? The abbey was built without cement, she told us; perhaps this was a folk memory of the earliest oratory on this spot, of the time of Kerry's Gallerus or Kilmalkedar, built in the dry-stone way. Some few cabins of this construction remain even now, almost undistinguishable from cow-byres except for a holy lamp, and most of the walls that divide the fields are open work against the sky, for if they met the winter gales with much resistance they would not stand.

By the time we left Mother Clancy's cottage, rain was falling heavily; it lashed our faces as we trudged along the exposed road between Toombeola and Roundstone. Usually the haunt of grey crows, this evening it seemed to be deserted even by these ill-omened birds. But we had another lucky lift, this time in a van, cards printed with images of the Sacred Heart and prayers for safety on the road hanging below the windscreen. We both squeezed into the front seat and were taken to the avenue of Letterdyfe.

Later in the evening the clouds parted, shafts of belated sunshine fell across the bay between masses of vapour as the showers shifted around the hills. Suddenly a magnificent double rainbow spanned the water, taking its rise from Roundstone jetty and plunging its further end into the unseen Well of the Seven Daughters on the opposite coast.

West to East

O NE EVENING B.Z. and I went with L. and N. in their
car to Dog's Bay, the next strand along the coast from
Gorteen. We struggled across the sand, windswept from
the west, paying little attention to its famous foraminiferous
qualities. The receding tide-line was scattered with hanks of
wrack and pieces of sea-soaked wood – windfalls is the Connemara name for flotsam and jetsam.

Once across the bay, we scrambled up the bleak headland
that juts beyond it, looking for a sheltered inlet from which to
bathe. Cattle tossed their horns and rolled their eyes suspiciously
at us; we continued across the peninsula till we reached the comparative shelter of Gorteen on the other side. Here the gapping
showers forced us under the lee of a sand-dune; inland, at the
back of us, Errisbeg was obscured by a curtain of cloud. Then
the sun came out briefly, transforming the grim landscape and
dissipating 'the mist that does be on the bog', and we bathed
in spite of the wind, climbing afterwards into our sopping
clothes. I was glad to accept a whiskey and soda from O. when
we returned to Letterdyfe.

The wind increased almost to gale force in the evening.
Ireland is at the mercy of the elements, and a sensitive human
being is at the mercy (if that is the right word) of elemental
waves of feeling – angst alternates with bitterness, an insane
gaiety with sorrow or timeless reverie. There are days when one
feels completely lost; the whole island seems lost, doomed to
be engulfed like Atlantis in mist and spray or blown away by
a gale from the ocean.

The high wind continued all night, torturing the trees around the yard where I was sleeping. Next day I walked in bright, violent weather to examine some large rocks on the way to the Inishnee turning. One was close to the Toombeola road not far beyond Letterdyfe – an immense granite block, roughly cone shaped from some angles of view, strong-stemmed ivy spreading a leafy cap on the top. The other, by the shore near the bridge, was a tower-like boulder also ivy-grown. I took it that both were natural formations – but this does not prevent an object of curious or striking shape from being invested in the popular mind with a supernatural numen. I made some drawings of them, climbing over the unsteady dry-stone walls and crossing smelly streams that drained into the estuary in order to obtain good views.

Later in the evening I went up to the copse beyond the rhododendron bushes above Letterdyfe and recited 'The Cold Heaven' and 'Sailing to Byzantium' into the wind. I could not ascribe my acute anxiety to any cause, whether of place, people or circumstance, but I think it was connected with my desire to go to the Aran Islands and the contrary feeling that I was not equal to the venture. The cold, the dubious outlook for weather and the stories I had heard about the discomfort of the boat that plies between Galway and the islands made me hesitate. I packed my possessions and decided at least to go to Galway next day with C. and E., who were driving there in any case. This would be much pleasanter than relying on the infrequent bus service.

By morning the wind had moderated but still blew from a grey sky. I determined to catch the afternoon train to Dublin. But Galway, when we arrived there, seemed warmer, and I again fell into a state of indecision. After a snack and drinks at the Great Southern, which had rather a friendly atmosphere for a large hotel, I felt I could have stayed there for a few days and perhaps even braved the crossing to Aran. But to go to Dublin seemed the way of least resistance, for Connemara had sapped my initiative to the point when I could scarcely make up my mind about anything. C. left the train at Mullingar to be met by a friend and driven to Slane.

The hotel where I found myself in Dublin was dark and depressing; there was no dinner, only high tea, a disastrous meal to which all Celtic countries except Brittany are addicted. When I see that group of sauce bottles on the table I know what to expect. I was tired so went early to bed and found that the water was barely tepid, so I could not have a bath. Nor could I sleep on account of the appalling noise of the traffic outside, but I must have dozed at last.

I awoke to a desperate morning, grey, damp and penetratingly cold. I wandered about St Stephen's Green looking for the statue of the Countess Markievicz but failed to find it. I was told later that it had been removed because someone had chipped the nose, and, being of limestone, it could not be repaired.

Exotic ducks were standing about the edge of a black pool, coloured prints being provided on a notice board to help one in identifying their species. A considerable interest in ornithology has grown of late years in Ireland, but I could feel no interest in these ornamental prisoners, who seemed as dispirited as myself.

A few weeks before, a memorial to the patriot O'Donovan Rossa had been erected in the park; the huge flattish rock set up on end was impressive, but the bronze plaque fastened on one side of it seemed trivial in contrast, and its portrait head in low relief showed but a shaky grasp of form. On the occasion of its unveiling, letters from his wife were quoted in the *Irish Times*, railing in embittered tones against the improvident ways of the born revolutionary: 'Who has the most reason to complain, I against you, or you against the authorities?'

Nearly all public notices are written in Irish as well as

English, including signposts and names of streets; even the lavatories are labelled *Mná* and *Fir*.

I called at Oona's flat; she was in, though hardly up. She showed not the least surprise at seeing me after an interval of years, though she was unprepared for my arrival, owing to a note having gone astray. She finished dressing and then helped me to find a quiet room in another hotel. But later I found there was a tank in it so had to move to the one above. I had been pursued by this hoodoo ever since coming to Ireland – at first, my room had backed on the bathroom, and at Letterdyfe my first night was made hideous by a sound like Niagara in the loft above me. Even after E. and C. had climbed into the roof and dealt with this, the tank would make peculiar explosive noises at intervals during the night, owing, it was said, to contraction, which often made me start from sleep.

It was terribly cold, and, as often happens in this country, the bedding felt damp. I put a fur jacket in the bed as a kind of mat to lie on and wrapped myself, above my usual nightwear, in a red wool cloak. I added another fur coat on top of the bedclothes and so managed to keep fairly warm.

Next day the weather was no better, the sky being so dark that the eclipse of the sun was scarcely noticeable. It is always depressing to come back to a town after a stay in the country, and somehow the sound of an itinerant musician, playing a bugle in dank Fitzwilliam Square, epitomized the whole of urban ennui and discouragement.

We lunched in one of those large popular restaurants where a trio still plays in the afternoon. Presently an old man sat down at our table; white hair fringed his enormous head, there was grime under his fingernails, his black clothes were greasy and ill kept. He would have liked to talk, I think, but Oona, shocked by his crude table manners and general grubbiness, was stonily disapproving. I took it that she knew him for a lunatic or bore; afterwards I was sorry that I did not at least pass the time of day.

I had tea with the Joseph Honeses at Leeson Park – he was W.B. Yeats's official biographer. I showed him my essay on Yeats's neglected masterpiece, *A Vision*, which he read most sympathetically, also photographs of my paintings. They had a geometric painting by the late Mamie Jellett, a friend of his cousin Evie Hone, the stained-glass designer.

In the evening Oona and I looked in for drinks at Davey Byrne's, the favourite bar with writers and artists. In the cocktail-lounge hung two paintings by Jack Yeats, one of them on the Ophelia theme which made me remember the aphorism of André Breton about Carrière who, he said, was 'surrealist in drowning'. We met a few people and were driven back in someone's car, rather drunk, to the Fergusons' flat, where we talked about Inishlackan and the west, Oona reliving some of her experiences on the island.

Next day I went to see Mrs Yeats and discussed my essay on *A Vision*; she made some useful criticisms, mainly in the pointing-out of factual errors. She insisted that I should note, in my own copy of the book, the few corrections which a new and forthcoming edition would contain. She often interviewed students, chiefly from India and the USA, who were taking her husband's work as subject for their Ph.D. theses. In the room hung paintings by Jack Yeats and a large stage design for *Deidre* by Robert Gregory.

Rathmines, the suburb where she lived, was rather like Turnham Green or Bedford Park, where Yeats himself lived when he first came to London with his parents.

In the evening I took Oona to the Gaiety Theatre to see *The Demon Lover* by Lennox Robinson. There were moments when the author seemed to be following Strindberg (though from a long distance), only to be succeeded by moments of sheer banality. The joints of construction creaked dismally – what had happened to a playwright well known in the heyday of the Abbey Theatre? The cast, with the exception of Hilton Edwards as the 'hero', might have been amateurs. Dublin's theatrical standards, once very high, have deteriorated and must be still dropping; this provincial approach was not so evident even a few years ago. The Abbey building, burned in 1951, was itself a great loss; those sad green walls and austere seats harboured a sense of excitement which communicated itself to even the poorest plays of later times.

I could not leave Dublin without seeing the bodies preserved in the vaults of St Michan's Church. This is a Protestant church of which there are actually more than Catholic in the city; the interior reminded me of Kirk Braddon in the Isle of Man, but the ceiling had a magnificent oval design in plaster. The air in the vaults is peculiarly dry for some reason, and this tends to preserve the corpses, though the flesh is desiccated and leathery. They are but skin and bone, tufts of faded hair clinging to one or two of the skulls. It is considered to bring good luck if one shakes the hand of one particularly large-boned corpse.

A similar necrophilic display could be seen in a Capuchin church in Rome, where the bodies of the brothers were preserved for centuries in the vaults. But, in contrast to the haphazard array of St Michan's, there a Latin love of pattern manifested itself; some of the bodies, clothed in their habits, were suspended from the walls and of those whose skeletons were no longer articulated the separate bones were set out in elaborate designs as though they had been pebbles or shells. But here the skeletal remains protruded half-heartedly from their coffins, draped in a dense wrapping of spiders' webs. It is a mystery what the spiders live on, for no other form of life inhabits the vaults. Outside, a grave is piously shown as that of the patriot Robert Emmet, and it may as well be here as elsewhere, since its situation is unknown.

In the evening I took a boat at the docks and stayed on deck for a while to 'feale the gay aire of my salt troublin bay and the race of the saywint up me ambushure'. Shafts of sunlight pierced the clouds from time to time, touching the Hill of Howth to the north, Joyce's 'HCE', 'Here comes everybody'. I looked for the 'buckgoat paps on him, soft ones for orphans' and in the skyline thought I saw them. Southward stood the red tower of the seamark that I had seen from the Wicklow coast when I went to Glendalough and the two Sugar Loaf Mountains beyond stretches of colourless smooth water. Iron objects that might have been sculptures of the school of Giacometti marked the channel until Dublin Bay was left behind.

Dublin Again

BELOW ME A vast landscape like snow fields, blue and gold, stretched as far as the eye could reach. The solider clouds had banked themselves into a range of hills beyond a furrowed cloud-plain, which opened into a crescent-shaped bay of sky. In the depth of this lagoon, like submarine vegetation and half veiled by filmier clouds, swayed the trees of the earth-map which formed its ocean floor. This country had its own horizon of cloud, far aloft from the horizon of earth, but, deceived by a view on two levels, I thought we were already flying over the Irish Sea. At 15,000 feet, the air was so pure that even an autumnal sun was dazzling.

Though a bad sailor, I am never airsick. I used to be nervous of flying, but now I would always choose it in preference to surface travel. The officials take care of one so well that one has a minimum of responsibility – one might almost be a package; and at 300 miles an hour the journey has no time to grow tedious.

I felt only a pleasurable excitement; the turbojet engine made such an impression of power that I was completely confident. We turned north as the clouds broke, and the Irish coast appeared in shadow beyond the shimmering sea, then we sank rapidly towards Dublin Airport. Even on earth the evening was fine, a clear light falling through the air of September's last days.

Next morning, as I was walking across Stephen's Green, an old beggar-woman from County Kerry hailed me. She told me that she was staying at a home for destitute people; it was not bad, she said, but it only gave shelter for the night, so she had to spend the day out of doors. In spite of the gathering cold, a bench on the green had become her sitting-room, all her possessions in an old sack at her side. She was hunting for a domestic job, she said, looking me over the while in a calculating fashion. She was rather dirty, her fingers much stained with nicotine; she asked me for twopence, which I readily gave her.

Dublin has many beggars. Later a tall, wild beggar-man was striding down Grafton Street dressed entirely in sacks. A family of beggar-children accosted me also, saying they would pray for me if I gave them money. Next day I again met the woman from Kerry; this time she proffered an empty cigarette box with an address scrawled on it, which she asked me to read for her. It was a place where she had to call about a job, she said, but I could not decipher all of it.

The weather having turned warm, I went for a walk along the city reaches of the Grand Canal near my lodging. The water was foaming beautifully through two locks and was crossed by an elegant small bridge, but the towpath was vestigial, and the water seemed scarcely to be used for freight. Canal traffic is picturesque but too leisurely, I suppose, even for Ireland in these days. The towns here still provide, however, a freer playground in their streets than do most places in England, because the volume of motor traffic is less large. Traditional rhymes and singing-games survive among the poorer children, and one occasionally catches an olden grace in little girls dancing on a pavement. One evening, while warmth still lingered in streets that had soon grown dusty through the dry spell, a group of them was playing some half-ritual game, their cries resounding persistently along the crescent. Their chanted refrain sounded like

> Naas, naas, naas, naas, naow!
> The king is goin' ta kiss ya
> The king is goin' ta kiss ya

Naas, naow, naas, naas, naow!
The king is goin' ta kill ya
Naas, naas, naas, naas, naow!

What might be the origin of this strange jingle – who was the king? Could it be a far-off echo of King William's invasion or of some yet earlier threat?

At the entrance to the National Museum stood a granite boulder from Hollywood in County Wicklow. Incised with a labyrinth pattern, it evoked the magic of the maze whose windings invite possessors of the clue to share their secret but defend their arcana from the profane, who may wander for ever in their circumvolutions.

I can never enter that circular hall containing the full-size reproductions of the chief high crosses without a keen feeling for the Irish countryside sweeping over me, for it is epitomized in the illuminated photographs of their sites. And in the galleries beyond, with their hoard of gold collars, torques and bracelets that have the same pale gleam as those from Mycenae, I feel a childish delight in archaeology as a treasure hunt. But this time I did not linger among them, and I passed the celebrated later works in silver or bronze – the Tara Brooch, the Ardagh Chalice, the Cross of Cong – with scarcely a glance, lovely though they are.

My attention was caught by the Kilnaboy Tau-Cross, which is almost certainly pre-Christian, each arm carved with a human head, and by the Corleek Trinity Stone, which is definitely pagan, though Christian instances of a similar iconography exist. The Corleek head is a multiple face rather than a complete trinity, since the eyes are not shared as they are, for example, in the head among the wood carvings of Sancreed church. These trinity heads, though tolerated in the early centuries of Christianity, were later condemned as blasphemous. Diagrams of the impossible, they exert on me a monstrous fascination as of a freak at a fair.

What is interesting in many ancient relics is the modification of their significance by time. Accident or the working of what I should once have called objective hazard has extended the process of their being from space into another dimension changing, but not weakening, their original intent. The wooden carving here from Ralaghan, Ireland's only prehistoric human figure in the round, recalls those in the Holderness boat. These were once unashamedly phallic, being designed for a part in some sexual rite, but the vicissitudes of the years have castrated them, and now they appear almost feminine. The Mên-an-Tol in Penwith, which once concealed its tomb structure under a heap of earth, now discloses, to all who can find it among the furze, a symbol of the eternal triangle. The Tolven Stone also, once the aperture through which a corpse was passed to rest in the tomb beyond, now gives an emblematic rebirth into wholeness, lifting from those who squeeze through it any disability of which they wish to be rid, from sterility to rheumatism.

Scattered about Kerry there are several pairs of massive pillars, which the country people call Gates of Glory. For the phantasy life of today, that is what they are, but who knows their original purpose? One can only guess that they had a ritual significance in some neolithic cult. Perhaps the most beautiful of them stands just outside the green bank surrounding the stone circle of Lissivigeen, seeming to guard the august ring of seven boulders within. Trees and bushes grow from this bank, though the central enclosure is clear of them, their branches cutting across the velvet-blue ridge of Killarney's mountains beyond. I have only seen this place at midday, but I can imagine that, viewed from the appropriate angle, either at sunset or dawn, its monolithic doorposts would not belie their name.

Night Life

THE GATE THEATRE was presenting *The Importance of Being Earnest* as a tribute to the memory of Oscar Wilde, whose centenary fell this October. Oona had obtained tickets through a friend of hers who worked in the production, so after a drink in the bar that used to be frequented by people from the old Abbey Theatre we went along to the Gate.

A kind of shrine had been set up in the foyer, centring on a photograph of the Anglo-Irish dramatist. It is odd that social disapproval has been mitigated to this extent during the last fifty years or so, while the law that condemned him remains unchanged.

I have never seen homosexuals in a London bar who flaunted themselves so blatantly (or was it gallantly?) as they did in Dublin. One evening we saw a group of them, its numbers continually swelled by new arrivals, drinking and gossiping in one of the principal bars. Powdered skin, blonded hair, languid or febrile gestures, eyes that slid glassily over women but kindled to a boy – these marked them out immediately. More still was their intonation unmistakable, penetrating the deeper tones of less exhibitionistic clients.

'He has the *most* lovely house, my dear, so you must pretend to be in love with him.'

Polite prostitution, discreet blackmail but, more corrupting than these, the cult of insincerity. The most degraded tart has too much integrity to pretend to be 'in love'; but is it, for many homosexuals, a choice between insincerity and insanity? One sensed a profound disquiet beneath their effrontery, and some of their jokes had a pathetic ring, a feminine identification carried almost to the extreme of hallucination – 'Darling, I must have a baby, *too!*'

Hostile comments from drinkers outside the confraternity had no suppressing effect; voices only rose more shrilly, postures became more exaggerated, phantasies more outrageous.

A friend of Oona's whom we met there asked me why some women liked to go about with 'queers'. I answered, rather stupidly, that I supposed they advised women on house furnishing, being interested in interior decoration. He cracked back at once that women should be more interested in central heating.

It was certainly Oscar Wilde who, more than anyone else, made the cult of insincerity socially acceptable with, alas, its dismal corollary: the idea that all amusing men are scoundrels and all reliable men bores. Apart from moral considerations, his influence has worked to vitiate perception, exalting talent above genius, the smart above the sublime.

As usual in the foyer Lord Longford, manager of Longford Productions, tall, plump and pink-faced, was leaning on a balustrade near an exhibition of his watercolour landscapes, a rickety charm perceptible through their uncertain technique.

The play was not badly acted, though the standard was far from metropolitan and the presentation lacked ideas – a symptom of the decline of the theatre in Ireland which I had noticed before. The new O'Casey play, *The Bishop's Bonfire*, put on after I left, has revived to some extent the traditions of other times, also the triple bill of the Abbey's Golden Jubilee – *On Baile's Strand* by W.B. Yeats, Synge's *The Shadow of the Glen* and Lady Gregory's *Spreading the News*. But taste and intellect have to struggle hard, for the band that mocked *The Playboy* is the band that rules the world in Ireland today, hence the fanatical censorship. One of the few points in favour of Partition is that banned books and contraceptives can be smuggled across the Ulster border.

I spent several mornings in the National Library, which is a good place for study, quiet but without formality. It would have been cold, sitting there for many hours, had not the weather been unusually genial. It was so fine that I longed to be out of the city and one afternoon managed to get as far as the Botanical Gardens. There was a sweet, damp smell in the glasshouses full of palms and orchids, offset by the more pungent scent of citrus fruits. Wandering through the formal park beyond, I chanced to go down by the stream and there heard sound of a scuffle. Half hidden in bushes, a couple stood swaying in an embrace, the man laying across the girl's buttocks with a stick. A more intense embrace followed.

In the evening Oona and some of her friends gathered at Sabrina's home in Ballsbridge. Her parents, evidently a wealthy middle-class couple by the look of the house, were away, leaving their arty daughter in charge. The spacious living-room was lit by candles, *cante jondo* poured from the radiogram, our tumblers were filled with red wine.

Soon Robert and Kate arrived with Bassie, then Joseph, Terence and Peter and lastly John. One end of the room had been cleared for dancing, and Robert, who had lived in Spain, began improvising dances with Sabrina while Kate beat time. In the intervals Sabrina kept filling up our tumblers; the night was freakishly close and still, so presently we all rushed out to the garden where there was a swing. Everyone swung on it in turn, but I refused, well knowing what the result would be. Then we found ourselves climbing the almost vertical stairway to an old stable which Sabrina had fixed up as a studio – I don't know how we managed the narrow treads without mishap – and looked at her paintings, though I have no clear recollection of what they were like.

We returned to the house for more drinks. While we were

outside the top of the piano had been burned by a falling candle and the pale carpet stained by upset wine – I pulled a settee over the spreading darkness. The radiogram was going through the Spanish records again, and we all danced, Joseph starting to bite people. And again we fled out to the mild night and the swing. The garden, now lit by a veiled moon, was quite extensive for a town house, but the neighbours must have been disturbed by our cries. Several of us climbed on the swing together, others pushing them so that they sailed up towards the trees, straining the strident ropes. We fell in a heap on the ground, swingers and swung, laughing wildly; I don't know who was on top of whom. Somehow we staggered back to the house.

Then Oona and Joseph, who had spent several summers on Inishlackan, sang a Connacht song and gave imitations of an islander they called the Bowsie – 'And the black wind in me arse'. They told stories of a madman there who had to be tied into a chair when the fit was on him but was soon going to be married, nevertheless. Next, Joseph, who was an excellent mimic, improvised a Cockney dialogue with Robert – an Ulsterman, though a Nationalist – on the theme of Ireland. John, who had been in ballet, began a solo, but Robert retired before this finished, and I found him at last lying alone and very subdued on the drawing-room sofa. He asked me to say a poem for him, but I could remember nothing.

Sabrina's generosity and good humour never wavered; our glasses were filled again before she vanished with Terence into the kitchen to cook supper. Towards two o'clock, sausages and bacon appeared, fried eggs and bread, and we spread the plates on the floor. John had collapsed into an easy chair and sat with his head in his hands while Kate coaxed him to eat. But the sight of food must finally have turned his stomach, and he had to dash away. I ate hungrily then almost fell asleep.

John had a car but was obviously in no shape to drive it; I don't know where he spent the night. Finally, Bassie, who had been unobtrusively drinking lemonade all the time, drove us home about four in the morning.

Near Drogheda

A FEW HOURS later I woke with a slight headache, which was not surprising. Luckily, it was the day of change from Summer Time, and, needless to say, I had not altered my watch the night before so had an unexpected hour in which to come to. Without this, I doubt whether I could have caught the midday train to Drogheda, but, as it was, I was able to make my rendezvous with Oona, who seemed little the worse for the party.

At no time did the railway run far from the coast, and this gave me good views of the Hill of Howth and the small island called Ireland's Eye just north of it. Then, beyond the village of Swords, we could see Lambay Island, noted for its bird sanctuary and subtropical vegetation. I have not been to Lambay, but I well remember Ilnacullin off Glengarriff during a warmer October than this, its vast rocks cloaked with exotic heaths and azaleas, palms and bamboos reflected in its ornamental water. But Glengarriff is on a sheltered inlet of Bantry Bay and is, in fact, the only place I have come across that has the supposed Irish 'softness' of climate. I find it difficult to believe that its profusion of growth can be equalled as far north and east as this.

We could see, too, the three little islands off Skerries as we raced on – it was a fast train – through Balbriggan and Gormanston, and we reached Drogheda in time for a late lunch at the house of Oona's sisters. In the evening, when we drove with Maire to the coast, we followed the valley of the widening Boyne for a little way, then turned north and, after meandering through lanes, reached the sea a little south of Annagassan.

The earlier drizzle had changed to fine weather with a tang in the air. Miles of stony sea wall edged the coastal meadows, dividing them from the shore; the tide was in, flapping quietly against the stones. There was no wide, lonely strand here as at Mornington, where the south side of the Boyne estuary curves into the sea coast. Enigmatic towers rise in that hinterland of dunes, their uses long forgotten. But here, looking to the north-east, we could see the heights bordering Carlingford Lough bleakly blue across the water and the Mountains of Mourne faintly discernible beyond, while inland the Cooley range, home of the Cuchullin Saga, showed darker and more clearly.

Oona and I wandered southward down the coast where an empty farmhouse gazed blankly out to sea through an imposing doorway with a window above, both nobly proportioned. In the flat fields around, the harvest was still in stooks, some of it even as yet uncut on account of the perishing summer.

I made sketches of some stagnant pools; these and the subtle forms of mudflats, laced with channels of water along an estuary laid bare by an ebb-tide, have a fascination for me. Such are the habitat of the waders and all birds of the foreshore.

When I was staying in Drogheda before, we visited Newgrange, most celebrated tumulus in Ireland. Set among the elms and lush grass of the Boyne Valley rose the green knoll overgrown with trees, bushes and ferns. A ring of unhewn rocks encircled it at a little distance with a rampart and ditch, and a kerb of huge slabs, some of them carved with spirals, retained the earth of the mound itself. A stone like these formed a lintel over the entrance, below which an iron grating had been fixed; we had to ask the custodian, who lived in a cottage near by, to unlock it before we could go in.

Art O'Murnaghan was with us; he loved to show people over the Brugh, as he always called it – though the term Brugh na Bóinne applies not to this one tumulus only but to the whole region. Since it was the palace of Angus Og, the Gaelic god of love and youth, the name Cashel Angus is more apt than Newgrange, for this latter was but the name given to the Georgian house built near it. The custodian provided us with candles, but Art dispensed with any further service from him and himself led us into the low-roofed passage.

The walls pressed uncomfortably close on either side, and as we crept along the height of the roof varied disconcertingly, dropping so low in two or three places that we had to crouch in order to move along at all. To those who take Cashel Angus as the Gaelic equivalent of the Great Pyramid, this passage into its depths was constructed as the setting for an initiation by ordeal or a symbolical death, therefore the obstructions were deliberate. To Art, this was certainly so; it was the centre of his religion. It is true that the way into the mound was made slightly easier by modern restoration, but whether the 'stumbling blocks' were originally intended or were the result of collapse in the course of ages it is difficult to say.

However this may be, we had not traversed more than half the length of the tunnel when I began to feel very strange indeed – as though the top of my head had been sliced off and no longer existed. I said I wanted to go back and would have done so but for Art, who encouraged me to continue, saying that the worst part was over. I think he would have been offended if one could not 'take' his beloved Brugh, and would have had a poor opinion of anyone whose nerve failed at the test.

So I struggled on, and, after what seemed a long time, the height of the ceiling rose decidedly, and we were in the central stone chamber. This was of beehive shape, about twenty feet high at the apex and as broad at the widest point and quite dark except for our guttering candles. Being roughly cruciform in plan, it was extended in three subsidiary cells or chapels, each with a large stone basin on the floor.

Art liked to meditate in the central chamber, which to him was a veritable vault of the adepts, but, though the quiet was impressive and the skilful stonework of the interior admirable, the dank air and enclosed feeling made me ill at ease. I was not sorry when we could retrace our way down the passage, though it seemed less formidable with daylight at the other end.

Like Gavrinnis in the Gulf of Morbihan and some of the larger mounds at Loughcrew, Cashel Angus had a definite opening which was at no time covered with earth or stones, and these entrances, like those of many ancient temples, faced eastward. None of these carns contained human remains, in this resembling the Great Pyramid; they may well have been temples rather than tombs. A church is not primarily a cemetery, though it may contain graves or its precinct be used for interments.

Perhaps the devotees at Cashel Angus imitated the sun's journey through the realms of darkness and sat or lay in one of its great basins, as Christian Rosenkreutz in the pastos or as the Egyptian adept in the Pyramid's stone chest. Or perhaps the mound symbolized for them not only the dead or dying Father, and hence the afterworld, but the womb of life, the producing Mother or the vagina of the Bride and hence the kingdom of the unborn. The whole place is a body image, and I never see plan drawings of such monuments without being reminded of the diagrams in a gynaecological textbook. This resemblance may be the result of objective hazard, the seemingly directed coincidence, a process now, I believe, more modishly known as synchronicity – a connection suddenly appearing, though not causally produced in time or space, and activated through some super-rational link.

There is a story that Angus brought the body of Diarmuid O'Dyna to this place after he was slain by the boar of Ben Bulben, for Diarmuid is both Tristan and Adonis. Angus could not restore him to life but was able to conjure a spirit into him so that they could talk together each day – an operation of necromancy which Tibetan wizards still claim to perform.

In *The Book of Ballymote*, this is the only one of the Boyne mounds designated a cashel. Two others are called dumas: one is the Mound of the Bones, which is probably Dowth, where human remains have been found; the other the Mound of Tresc, which may be Knowth. The other monuments listed – there are over twenty of them – seem to be put into a different class, and without doubt many of these were tombs.

We went on to Dowth, which was only about a mile distant, that same day; the mound was much less conspicuous than Cashel Angus, being overgrown with furze. More than one passage penetrated its depths, and the tunnels were twisting, though much shorter; there were several side chambers and at the entrance two cells of later date. In general, the workmanship was rougher than that of Cashel Angus and the carved stones fewer.

In no megalithic carving that I have seen have I been able to trace the supposed representational element. The forms seem to me abstract if not strictly geometric in character, and I cannot help thinking that when archaeologists see in them human faces or figures, boats, leaves or other objects it is usually a case of projection, like seeing pictures in the fire. Not that the artists were mere pattern-makers, but, to them, each form symbolized something that could be recognized, though their glyphs were not realistic, so modern interpretations are probably far astray.

Another time we visited Monasterboice, when a serene chilly evening in May was turning from grey to gold, the sun sinking into a luminous haze. The round-tower in the graveyard was topless, a symbol of castration, but three masculine crosses carried the image over into a new epoch in a more complete disguise. The almost-level rays transformed the grey and green of the deserted cemetery into the colours of stained glass or illumination – the light being golden, the shade side and interiors transparent red, the cast shadows a rich blue.

The high crosses were perhaps the finest in Ireland. Some think that they were erected, here as elsewhere, at the eight chief compass points on a more or less circular periphery with the church as centre, thus forming a kind of three-dimensional mandala. At Kells, at Glendalough, at Clonmacnoise and elsewhere traces of such a magically guarded precinct remain. Here, the West Cross by the round-tower was the tallest, but Muiredach's Cross the most elaborately carved. On the lower panel of one of its arms a monstrous hand was sculptured, bringing to mind the Hand of Fatima used everywhere, in jewellery no less than in architectural motif, as North Africa's talisman against the Evil Eye. The East Cross was much broken and little carved but stood apart from the other remains with a certain sad dignity.

Of the two ruined churches there, neither had the power of that hidden rectangle, its walls overgrown with moss and grasses, its entrance almost impassable with thorns, which I once found on the island of Inisfallen at Killarney. On the green altar a single dandelion grew to the right, a single huge daisy to the left, so I called it the Chapel of the Sun and Moon.

Grey ruins of Mellifont, too, I remembered, the 'honey-fountain' beside the river Mattock. It was once a Cistercian abbey, but Ireland's earliest Gothic was now sunken in banks of nettles. Half the worn octagonal baptistery remained, and a small church in the valley below, seemingly deserted, caught the eye, though unconnected with the abbey.

On one of the old walls in Drogheda was carved a sheela-na-gig, an imp-like figure sitting cross-legged to propitiate the goddess of fertility. When we returned, twilight was fast falling, and we found tinker women sitting on the kerb outside. Maire did not encourage their custom in the bar because other clients objected to their dirtiness, and quarrels often broke out when the excitable tinker men 'had drink taken'. We talked to them and tried to make sketches, though they did not attempt to keep still. One had wide cheekbones, a dark skin and tow-coloured hair, as many of them have; her little girl was exactly like her. The other must, by her blue eyes, blue blouse and pearly ear-rings, have been an avatar of Mary Gyp, the May Bride, sea goddess and muse. She had the same look as the gypsy who came once to the door in Athens selling coffee mills and conjured luck for me from a glass of water. But this one's features were more beautiful, and even the curve of her wrist as she held a nipple to her infant's mouth was full of natural grace.

It seemed, from what they told us, that they had a more or less permanent camp beside the Boyne and just beyond the outskirts of the town, and they asked us to visit them there. Blessings were called down on us for our gift of silver. These women were poor but hardy; they were indifferent to the cold as they sat waiting for who knows what on a kerbstone in the misty dusk.

The Hag's Mountain

N EXT MORNING OONA, Peggy and I set out for
Loughcrew. Though our road led through Slane and
Kells, we had not time to do more than glance at them
as we drove through, but we passed the famous high cross, used
as a gallows after the rebellion of '98, in the marketplace of Kells
and on the western outskirts the topless round-tower with five
look-out openings instead of the usual four, commanding the
five ancient approaches to the town.

The monastic settlement of Kells was founded by St
Colmcille and strengthened later by refugee monks from his
ravaged foundation at Iona. Its scriptorium produced the
illuminated gospels in Latin universally known as *The Book of
Kells* and now treasured in the library of Trinity College. This
masterpiece was not always appreciated, for it was found lying
on a midden near Slane, bereft of its covering shrine, which
had been stolen for its jewel work. The combination of abstrac-
tion and phantasy in the decorations is unique and of a technical
virtuosity so fine one can hardly believe it to be the work of
human beings. It seems rather to have been precipitated by
some magical means – even the colour recalls that of dream
life rather than of physical reality. Incidentally, the half-Uncial
alphabet in which it is written is probably the oldest cursive
script in the world and was brought to England by the Irish
monks of Lindisfarne and other foundations. It was only

superseded by the French script in Norman times, so in a sense England owes to Ireland her first literacy.

We were looking for the road to Oldcastle but somehow missed it and found ourselves climbing steeply into cloud. On the crest of a hill we stopped and looked down to the plain on the far side; we must have been at the eastern end of the Loughcrew Hills, near the summit called Carnbane but some distance from the main approach to its antiquities. A standing-stone, or *gallán*, loomed out of the mist on the hillside to our left, but we did not examine it. We retraced our way to the base of the ridge and then turned westward. Soon we saw a notice directing us to 'Tumuli and Carns'; we parked the car in the muddy lane and had a picnic lunch on the bonnet, borrowing cups from a cottage near by.

A misty rain was falling but not wetting us as we scrambled up the boreen. We looked back over the plains of Meath, where smoke-blue hills showed up clearly in the distance with two crook peaks – mountains of Offaly or Kildare perhaps, for they could hardly be outliers of the Slieve Bloom. Just below lay the wooded parklands surrounding Loughcrew House; in some part of the demesne was the birthplace of Blessed Oliver Plunkett, martyred at Tyburn. I had seen his mummified head resting, illuminated like a work of art, in a glass box on a Drogheda altar, an instance of the grisly fetishism of Catholic relics. Once it was housed in a convent school of the neighbourhood, but it got a worm in it and had to be treated. Now, though the eyes are mere slits and the hairless skin darkened and desiccated, it shows no sign of decay.

The tiny lough of Loughcrew glistened in the foreground just beyond the road; its Irish name means the Lake of the Spreading Tree, and probably once referred to some tree sancti-fied by rite. Many of the smaller green hills near by had a rounded look as though artificially built up or altered – as might well be, since the neighbourhood was full of ancient remains.

As we faced upwards, a hill bathed in a mysterious atmosphere stretched sleepily to our left where a row of giant thorn trees, their berry-laden twigs glowing with a subdued crimson, bordered an abrupt green slope. Above this, a craggy hillside rich with the colour of sodden autumnal fern met a sky that seemed part of the earth, lifting for a moment and then coming down again with a dew that scarcely wetted. More than many places in the celebrated west, this country had an enchanted air; it might have been the setting for James Stephens's *Crock of Gold*.

The boreen led to a pass between the two main summits of the ridge, the Hag's Mountain proper and Patrickstown Hill; a man who had been loading timber on a tractor told us to take the path to the left for 'the caves'. I asked him whether the cattle roving across the mountainy pastures were harmless, and he replied that we'd be 'dead safe' with them. Once on the path the going was very bad, the pale brick-coloured mud inches deep, and the hill crests in front of us, though less than a thousand feet high, were wrapped in mist.

The name of the whole range is Sliabh-na-Caillighe, the Hag's Mountain, and it is named after that haunter of Gaelic heather, the Hag who is also the Maiden. In Ireland she first appeared, perhaps, as the triple Banba-Fódla-Ériu goddess of the land who, in her third aspect, married the sky god Lugh at Tailteann, not far from here. For long afterwards, annual fires were lighted there in their honour on 2 August. Both sister and bride of the sun, she was earth fruitful to the plough and yet crone also, breeder of enchantments, beldam of the hazel wand. Later she appeared among Ireland's demigoddesses, degraded by Christianity to Hags – Babh, Ainé and Beara. Babh was a kind of multiple war-goddess, herself subdivided into three aspects as Neman, Macha and the Morrígan, but Ainé and Beara were beneficent.

Of Beara they said that in old age she again became youthful, renewing herself like the moon, that 'her children were tribes and races' and that for lovers she had heroes and gods. She outlasted them all; seven times did the rags of age fall from her till Cumine put the nunnery veil on her head. In *The Lament of the Hag of Beare*, translated by Stephen Gwynn, she calls these changes tides:

> Ebbing, the wave of the sea
> Leaves, where it wantoned before
> Wan and naked the shore
> Heavy the clotted weed:
> And in my heart, woe is me!
> Ebbs a wave of the sea.
>
> I am the Woman of Beare
> Foul am I that was fair:
> Gold-embroidered smocks I had,
> Now in rags am scarcely clad.

And, though she is singing at the ebb, surely the flow must have returned, carrying from her the conventual white and black and bringing again the golden weeds.

Off the coast of Bantry Bay lies a rocky islet ringed with orange-coloured sea wrack that perpetuates her name, and she has left many traces over the countryside. Hidden behind the Twelve Bens is a hill called the Cailleách, and near Monasterboice is a gallery grave which is still pointed out as her house. Here, above us, a megalith has become the Hag's Bed. In a later legend it is told how the tall Beara was leaping one day from peak to peak of the Loughcrew range in accomplishment of a magical operation, her apron full of stones. Some of these fell, forming carns, circles, monoliths and stone alignments. Some say that afterwards she rested on her 'bed'; others that she fell while jumping and, like Umm Harâm, the Prophet's aunt, broke her neck and so found here her tomb.

Sometimes she was petromorphic, a female herm, and, from being a stone herself, she converted stones into men. Or, Gorgon-like, she turned men into stones – those rings of petrified dancers, those ranks of unmoving men-at-arms, are the Hag's work. But, again like the Gorgons, she was a sea divinity, never far from the rush of water in whose tumult oracular voices might be heard. Visions, too, might be seen in the swirling depths where reflections from the surface mingled with shadows falling athwart a translucent eddy full of weed. And sometimes she hid in the last swathe to be reaped or the last shock to be tied and was called, when fashioned into a strawy puppet, both Maiden and Granny.

Perhaps she still lingers in the country's inner life, showing herself on occasion as a warning sprite, the banshee of a family – like Ivel of Craglea to the Dalcassians – or the dreaded Washer of the Ford. She is one of the Great Invisibles; Cathleen-ni-Houlihan is both the Colleen Bawn and the Shan Van Vocht, the 'poor old woman'. Her moods still inform the caprices of climate and vegetation and who knows what else that we see, for the apprehensible world helps her to manifest. Taking from sea, stone and corn, moon, earth and the unearthly abysses, she has left memorials throughout the Celtic west.

Where should one assign her in the pantheon of the Tree of Life? Jesod is the moon and so the Triple Goddess; Malkuth the earth mother and favourer of corn – any manifestation of fertility. The Hag subsumes both these but perhaps should rather be ascribed with Hecate and the governess of floods to the sphere of Jesod.

The first carn we came to was a circular pit lined with upright stones crowning a hill. The second was more complete, of the type of Cashel Angus but smaller – a mound retained by horizontal slabs with an entrance towards the east now partly overgrown by thorny sloes and a court or passage leading to it faced with stone uprights and a kind of stone stile across it. No doubt the whole mound was once, like Cashel Angus, covered with shining quartz pebbles. The construction of the interior was decadent cruciform with two side chambers, many of the uprights and lintels inscribed with indecipherable designs.

To the west and a little lower on the hill we saw a flattened circular mound fenced with stones; to the south on a rising peak a higher carn with a large stone outside it loomed out of the mist. This must have been that traditionally called the Tomb of Ollamh Fodhla and also ascribed to his descendant, Concubar, King of Ulster. Ollamh Fodhla was a great jurist of the Brehon system and a Druid, too, as all such law-givers were; the Hag's Bed is called his chair, some saying that it was a kind of throne used at inauguration ceremonies. But this is an invasion of Beare's territory, for the rock scribings are mainly of feminine form – circles single or concentric or cup-shaped surrounded with a ring. The legendary connection with Queen Tailté is more apposite, for she is but the Hag in another guise: she is said to have married a Firbolg king, Eochad Mac Erc, and to have been buried with him on this mountain – forerunner in myth of that later story of Lugh and Ériu.

The Loughcrew Hills were certainly the cemetery of Tailteann where the famous games were yearly held in her honour. It was, like Cruachan and the Brugh of the Boyne, one of the great cemeteries of Gaeldom. But the cult was not only a cult of the dead, and Cashel Angus was not primarily a tomb. The Loughcrew carns may be older than Cashel Angus, and though many of the smaller ones were undoubtedly graves two or three of the larger were no more so than Cashel Angus itself.

In the fading light it was difficult to make out the rock-cut designs, but they seemed to consist of a small number of two-dimensional forms, mainly calligraphic in character and but lightly inscribed. Their purpose was evidently symbolic rather than decorative; one carving can be seen only by looking through a narrow aperture in the stone, suggesting that it should be ritually viewed by a certain person or at specified times. There must have been a magical intention on the part of the craftsman or, rather, of the priest who directed him; artistic self-expression, as understood today, would have been unknown.

A feeling of uneasiness began to invade me, whether due to the enclosed interior of the tumulus, the semi-darkness within and the fall of twilight without, the thickening of the mist or the restlessness of the castle on the hillside, I cannot tell. But there was an eerie quality in the quiet, a hint of the Hag's presence brooding over the place, now alluring the climber to mount to her abode, now repulsing the one who ventured too far.

Veils of mist were driving in from the west, and the cattle were moving in a disturbed way. I am always nervous of horned beasts in haunted places – panic may easily descend upon them. Remembering the disquiet of the herds near the Witches' Mill at Castletown in the Isle of Man and that story by Saki called 'The Music on the Hill', I felt that anything might happen. The mist was by this time so thick that had we explored further we should have been unable to find our way down. So we descended, and once away from the highest carns the haze not only thinned out but the tension in some less-palpable atmosphere was eased.

Loughcrew is an isolated ridge with a wide view of the plain to north and south. Once there were more than fifty carns here, but now fewer than thirty remain. Before the days of the serious archaeologist many of their stones were pillaged for building purposes – though if superstitious awe prevented such desecration in some places, one wonders why it did not operate here? It seems to be an emotion of haphazard incidence, some-times possessing all the force of a primitive taboo, sometimes so weak as to be easily disregarded by the pushful or the rapacious.

A round, fort-like structure could be seen just below us near a cornfield with the harvest still in stooks, and a green rampart rose above another cornfield on the northern scarp of the hill. One could spend weeks wandering among the antiquities here.

But darkness was gathering, and we made our way down to the car. In the grass beside the track I found a dying rabbit, blind and hideously swollen, a victim of myxomatosis. We had read in the local paper of farmers paying a high price for infected animals in order to spread the disease on their land, and there was even a report of tinkers putting pepper in rabbits' eyes to pretend they were infected and so obtain the money. Driving back in the wet, the rain lessened as we approached Drogheda; the weather is drier on the east coast, but every eminence on the central plain catches the cloud.

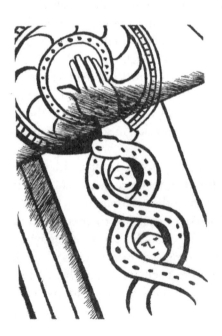

Knowth and Slane

ONA AND I were driving through the park-like country of the Boyne Valley; an easterly breeze was chasing massive clouds across the blue, but the sun shone serenely on the season's withdrawing life.

Soon we had left County Louth and entered Meath; we were making for the tumulus of Knowth, leaving aside the more famous sister mounds of Dowth and Newgrange, which we knew already. We followed a curving road on the northern side of the Boyne and soon drew up beside a field on our left. Some steps led up the wall that bordered this field, and here we sat to eat our lunch with the mound just the other side.

Behind us and on the opposite side of the road stood Knowth House, now empty and closed. It was what the agents call a 'gentleman's residence', in the Georgian style and attractive but for its north aspect. We remembered meeting the woman who used to live there and her young son when we were looking over Dowth on the day we visited the Boyne antiquities with Art O'Murnaghan. She had since left and gone to Australia, her invalid husband having died, but at the time she had seemed much intrigued with Art's esoteric theories. This was one of the two houses of some pretension situated near these Bronze Age tumuli, this one at Knowth and the New Grange at Cashel Angus.

Cattle, young bulls perhaps, were setting across the pasture surrounding the mound of Knowth with that automatic yet purposive drift which seems to be directed by the group soul of a herd. We waited for this urge to take them some little distance away before climbing the tumulus ourselves. Knowth had none of the hieratic dignity of Cashel Angus nor the bosky retired charm of Dowth. It was simply a bare green dome, but crowning the steep above the Boyne's north bank where the river makes a great loop, it shows as a striking landmark when seen from below on the opposite shore. Oona had previously made a painting from this view as part of her re-creation of the Boyne country. Though locally called King Cormac's Grave, it was not, so far as is known, a grave at all and belonged to a time far earlier than that of Cormac Mac Art, King of Tara, who actually was buried at Rossnaree on the southern bank. Such popular ascriptions of monuments are not unusual; there is a horned carn in the Isle of Man known as King Orry's Grave, which is said to have been the resting place of a giant king. Orry, though a half-legendary ruler of the island, was much later in date than his supposed tomb.

Knowth had never been thoroughly explored, but the summit bore traces of archaeological prospecting. No entrance to a passageway was found, though, on the analogy of Dowth and Cashel Angus, one would expect it here also. A retaining wall of stones carved with designs in the tradition of the other tumuli was said to encircle the base, but to us they were invisible, being completely covered with earth and grass. A few ancient-looking stones were lying about in the vicinity, one in the hedge to the left, another projecting from the side of the mound itself a little way up. From the top, a sunlit expanse of Meath lay below us, pale ruins on the Hill of Slane showing up vividly to the west.

We wandered down the meadows towards the river; a little below Knowth and to the left, traces of what might have been earthworks appeared – perhaps the remains of Dowth Castle, said to be in this neighbourhood. We had vague thoughts of looking for a path to Newgrange but decided that this would take us too far away from the car.

Above the precipitous bank, matted with close-growing scrub, we could hear the rush of water and catch a glimpse of silver – a wide bend of the Boyne below us. At hand, a stream oozed seemingly from the roots of an ash tree, and there was a tantalizing air of enchantment about the unspectacular thorn hedges, muddy tracks and fading ferns. A holy well was situated just about here, so I learned later – perhaps it was the very spring at the base of the tree, though no stone coping was visible. The foundations of a medieval church were not far off and a souterrain, but these remained undiscovered by us. We were not even looking for them, being unconscious of their existence, but we were looking for something, we did not know what, and were drawn by their hidden influence.

But we could wait no longer if we wanted to see Slane before dark, so we persuaded Oona's car to start by pushing it from behind and letting it run downhill. A few miles further, and we were in a delightful little street of Georgian houses with the walls enclosing the great trees of the Conyngham demesne beyond. On the day of the Assumption this park is still thronged with people who come to take water from Our Lady's Well.

We turned to the right in the middle of Slane village and went up a steep hill; we left the car on the main road and continued upwards on foot. Evening damp was already rising to our nostrils, though the sky was still bright. On the brow of the hill we crossed a sloping pasture where more cattle were stravaguing about; we were in some doubt as to their sex, Oona inclining to the view that they were heifers. To me their anatomy looked different from that of most heifers, and I took them for bullocks. Whatever they were, they seemed restive, and I was glad to get through the wicket in the wall surrounding some of the ecclesiastical remains.

The ruins of the square tower with a graceful arch rose up before us, silhouetted against the burnished sky; at our feet lay the tombs of forgotten scholars. From this, the highest point of the hill, St Patrick must have lighted the paschal fire on that fireless night before Beltane to supersede the pagan blaze of Tara. Though this beacon of defiance failed to convert the king, it signalled the beginning of the end for Tara's glory – with the spread of Christianity its importance waned, and triumph shifted to the Hill of Slane. Tradition says that St Patrick, to commemorate his gesture, founded a monastery here; certainly the more recent Franciscan house occupied the site of an earlier foundation.

The remains of the convent buildings were grouped a little apart from the church – we slipped across the intervening green without attracting the attention of the cattle. Once inside I felt safer, as the doorway seemed too narrow for them. Roofless walls enclosed us, on one of which vestiges of a rough carving could be seen, its theme indecipherable. To the east these had a suggestion of defence, and as we gazed from their massive bastions, the Boyne Valley from Drogheda to Trim lay open below, with the pastures of Meath stretching southward to Tara's hill.

As the light grew more golden, I could feel the pull of something older to the west. We left the monastic precinct and climbed through a barbed-wire fence beyond the church into a deserted field. The grass was no longer close-cropped but lay in rain-drenched swathes; had it been upright it would have stood waist high. Ahead, shafts of levelling sunlight fell between the trunks of chestnut trees, making their leaves transparent. The woodland seemed to be hiding some focal point of force which drew me towards it yet at the same time repelled. Fear was pressing me backwards, as though from a defended place; I scanned the field for any sign of dangerous beasts, but there was none. The hedge to the right had several gaps, but the field beyond was also empty – the menace had some less tangible source. My boots sinking into the heavy grass and fallen leaves, I strode on, determined to storm this outpost of autumn.

Masked by the trees and undergrowth was a steep mound encircled with a ditch. It was about the same size and shape as Ward Castle, a vitrified fort in the Isle of Man. We scrambled through the bushes up to its flattened summit, also tree-grown; glimpsed through the wooded hillside below the mound, the plains seemed filled with golden mist. Perhaps it was on this eminence that St Patrick lit his fire, for it was higher than any ground we had passed over and would be better seen. Thus would he have adopted a pagan site as well as a pagan rite for his own announcement.

On our way downhill towards the village we stopped to examine a tower like a large dovecot next to a modern church; it may have once been a bell tower separate from an older structure and, though retained, no longer in use.

As we returned in the twilight along the south side of the valley, we came upon a tinker family cooking their evening meal by the roadside. We stopped to speak with them and give them money; we asked, too, if we might make drawings of them, which they were very pleased for us to do. It is likely that they were agreeably surprised at any show of friendliness, for most people despise and distrust them so much that they will hardly give them a good evening.

We soon discovered that they were not, in any conventional sense, a family; the man and woman were not married, and the little girl was not the woman's child, though she may have been his. We could not make out whether the three boys were theirs. He was a wild-mannered man, shouting the woman down if she tried to join in the talk, putting on an act to impress us that he had been in the British Army. But when he told us his name and where he lived when in Drogheda, Oona recognized him as belonging to a notorious family, his brother seldom out of gaol. The woman also tried, naïvely enough, to impress us with her respectability, telling us she had a job in Navan, but it would be an unlikely thing if either got employment. Except for bad teeth, however, they looked healthy enough, their faces weathered to a brick colour and their hair darkened with grime.

The children, too, looked splendid and were evidently enjoying this rough life on the roads where they were never washed or combed. One of the boys was a little *farouche* and stood apart or leaned on his bicycle without saying a word. Another was attending to a cooking-pot of blackened iron hung over the fire by a hook. This contained bones half immersed in greasy water with, I suppose, a few root vegetables stolen from neighbouring farms; but this fare, however meagre, must have agreed with them. The little girl was a beauty; the smears on her face could not hide her brilliant skin or dust dim her red-gold curls.

An open tent with old coats serving as a groundsheet was prepared for their night's lodging. A few yards away stood their cart, the donkey that drew it browsing in the hedge. We asked Michael, the youngest boy, if we could sketch him, and he came forward, shy and respectful, pulling off a battered cap to reveal his mop of sandy hair. He had so much the same high cheekbones and pointed chin as the girl that we thought they must be brother and sister. But who could guess what wind of destiny had blown them all together, so that they shared a life of travelling the roads? Whatever the children missed in schooling they made up for in self-reliance; we saw that they were as much at home in the countryside as hedge sparrows and almost as well able to fend for themselves.

'*Beannact-leat!*' shouted the man as we took our leave. '*Dia-linn!*'

Tara of the Kings

I AM GLAD not to be an archaeologist, for my lack of status allows me simply to enjoy myself among antiquities. I can interpret them according to my own morphological intuitions without reference to current orthodoxies or deference to any school of thought – even without strict regard to evidence.

On our way to Tara we noticed a round-tower standing beside a ruined church in the tree-grown graveyard of Donaghmore. As is usual, its door was placed high above ground, lending colour to the accepted theory of the round-towers as places of refuge; and its keystone was carved with a crucifixion scene, supporting the contention that they are of Christian origin. And yet – I had already seen examples at Glendalough, Aghadoe, Monasterboice, Clondalkin and Kells, and I could not wholeheartedly accept this polite and utilitarian explanation – even if the actual structures dated from the Christian era, how far had the new religion penetrated by then? Is not their latent intention to manifest once more the worldwide cult of the linga? This is their meaning at dream level, whatever may have been their uses. Even their date may be doubtful, for there are cognate structures in other lands – the *broch* in Scotland and its counterpart in Sardinia – of much earlier date than Ireland's Viking raids. That some remembrance at least of a fire-and-serpent cult was built into the later towers, I feel sure.

Soon we were in Navan, An Uaimh – the Grotto is the picturesque meaning of the name – belied by the appearance of a characterless market town huddled under the clouds and giving little hint of its former historic importance. But the name made me suspect the presence of underground chambers like those of the Brugh and Sliabh-na-Caillighe, still locally called caves and may actually refer to the souterrain at Athlumney near by.

Seminarists going for a walk along the high road in twos and threes, 'mothers' boys' for the most part, earnest and spotty-chinned, made us aware of Dundalgan hidden in trees to our right up a long avenue. An iron curtain had already descended to divide these youths from the life of the country-side through which they trudged – having been told, no doubt, that exercise was 'good for them' – and an equally resistant veil had set in their psyche a limit on speculation and the right to explore.

Our road approached the Hill of Tara from the back – that is, from the east where it had least elevation, so that we arrived on a scene lacking in drama if not without charm. A tiny village of four or five houses, one with a shop and the usual bar, then a gentle slope, grass-covered, a church and churchyard to the left, and we were standing in the Enclosure of the Synods. Once surrounded by a triple bank, this was the scene of three synods, convened respectively by St Patrick, St Ruadhán of Lorrha and St Adamnan, disciple of Colmcille. But now even its situation was difficult to trace, for the earthworks were badly damaged last century when an obscure sect – an adherent of which is said to live still in the neighbourhood – excavated the enclosure supposing the Ark of the Covenant to be buried here. Needless to say, this valuable relic remained undiscovered.

In those days, any self-styled antiquary could dig without hindrance and without possessing any archaeological knowledge; in consequence, many sites were spoiled for better-qualified research. It is only of recent years that this haphazard scratching has been forbidden, Éire having taken seriously its trusteeship of the past. Official investigation was begun on the Enclosure in 1952, but the results are still unpublished.

My own antiquarian musings, however unpalatable to the orthodox, at least do no material harm. The fascination which any ancient enclosure exercises over me may perhaps be explained by a race memory going back into the earliest times. The marking out of a space of ground symbolizes, I suppose, the first hint of civilization, a something distinguished deliberately from the wild, the original temenos. The immediate purpose seems unimportant – I cannot even see children designing an oblong in the sand as an imitation sports ground without an atavistic pang. A hint of ceremony is never absent from this marking out, as of a performance about to begin, whether an acrobatic display or the founding of a city.

A modern wall cut across the hill, on the far side of which we found the Fort of the Kings, whose area occupied the whole summit. But the encircling ditch was shallow and the bank low, since grazing and perhaps cultivation at some period had tended to level them. There was nothing spectacular at Tara like the vallum at Avebury or the ditches of Maiden Castle, but it exhaled its own impalpable atmosphere, quiet and sad, which seeped into the consciousness and gradually made its effect.

Within the precinct, the most obvious structure was the steep-sided Mound of the Hostages, which perhaps entombed the remains of sureties slain because of their overlord's failure in tribute to the High King. West of this lay a series of ditch-and-rampart formations which in plan made a maze-like pattern or dual circle, linked in serpentine fashion with smaller rings or parts of rings within. The two main circles were traditionally called Cormac's House and the Royal Seat; the latter was described by MacAlister as pre-dating the former, having been the dwelling of kings earlier than Cormac Mac Art, but in plan the two seemed inseparable. The Royal Seat has not, apparently, been excavated, so the dating may yet be revised.

It was only possible to guess at the purpose of these structures, but knowing that the High King was by no means a purely secular figure but as much priest as warrior and law-giver, one might guess that the kind of defence which these curving banks represented was as much magical as military in intent.

Though the scene of an ecclesiastical synod on three occasions at least, it was as a centre of unchristened Gaeldom that Tara flourished. This pagan aura still clung about its green earthworks in spite of the plaster statue of St Patrick – in the feeblest Catholic-repository style – which shared the railed-off centre of Cormac's House with the Lia Fáil. The pretext for the modern uprising of this ancient stone was to mark the grave of those killed in the '98 rebellion, and so it was removed from the place where it had long lain on the Mound of the Hostages. Since this was the traditional site of the inauguration ceremonies, the five-foot pillar now standing on Cormac's House may well have been the identical stone then used, though there is also a story that the Stone of Scone came originally from this spot. The Lia Fáil was waiting under the change-ful evening sky for a libation of oil, but this was replaced by a light shower.

Legend endowed many standing-stones with animation; in some localities they piped and danced, in others they went down to a river to drink, and they often spoke. Here the Lia Fáil was said to scream at the climax of the inauguration of a rightful king, as the Stone of Scone was believed to roar. It would be interesting to know whether the microphone picked up any rumbling at the Coronation in 1953.

Southward, beyond the encirclement of the Fort of Kings, we looked for King Laoghaire's Fort, but so sunken were its ramparts that we could scarcely trace their position. At the time when St Patrick landed in Ireland, Laoghaire was ruling the country, and tradition says that he was buried here.

As we walked back along the crest of the hill, we looked down on the vast expanse commanded by Tara to westward; to the north we could see the mountains of Cavan in the distance and the nearer eminences of Slane and Loughcrew, sometimes hidden by scuds of rain. Clouds were blowing in from the west, but we did not heed them nor hurry as we ranged back towards the north-eastern quarter of the hill to see the Banqueting Hall.

The foundations of this were over 700 feet long, a huge size for a structure in wood, as were all Tara's buildings – hence their vanishing without a trace. Each rank, trade and profession of the ancient world had here its allotted alcove; among these was a place for harpers, so it was through this hall that 'the soul of music' was shed. There were entrances at either end and six doors along each side.

Its size was especially necessary on the occasion of the three-yearly *Feis*, or festival – founded, it is said, by that Ollamh Fodhla sometimes associated with Sliabh-na-Caillighe – when Tara became the scene of a combined eisteddfod, Olympic Games, church assembly and parliamentary session. It was the centre of the Bardic life pattern which did not distinguish sharply between these varied functions. From the third century till the sixth, it was the seat of Ireland's High Kings – the name Teamhair na Riogha means Acropolis of the Kings – and remained in some sort a royal centre until the death of Malachi II in 1022.

Further on we came to the Fort of Gráinne whose name recalls that famous story on the Tristan theme, *The Pursuit of Diarmuid and Gráinne*, in which the hero Finn MacCool corresponds to the outraged King Mark, Gráinne his errant bride to Isolt and Diarmuid to the lieutenant who elopes with her. Gráinne was the daughter of Cormac Mac Art, the first High King, and, though these half-effaced foundations still recalled the Ossianic legendary cycle, no mound marked the resting place of an earlier cycle's hero, Cuchullin, whose head and hand were brought to Tara by his enemies for burial after the Battle of Slieve Fuad.

Sparse woodland now began, beeches and chestnuts growing from the green abraded ditches where the scarp of the hill fell steeply away. We continued through this belt of copseland looking for the Calf's Well and the site of Cormac's Kitchen. The slope on our right exhaled the scents of autumn and the poignancy of damp evening air; the same atmosphere as hung over the tree-covered fort on the Hill of Slane was perceptible here. When the trees thinned away at the far end and we had still not found either ráth or well, we crossed a field beyond, looking again at the map. We peered through a hedge on the other side and saw the spot where they must once have been, though there was no longer a trace of the 'kitchen' and, of the well, only a slight marshiness of the ground.

Climbing the hill-brow again, we skirted the Fort of the Kings and entered the modern churchyard sheltered by trees. Here stood the so-called Cross of Adamnan, older far than Christianity and so broken that it was hard to say whether it had been at any time cruciform. A figure, just discernibly carved on the eastern face, has been identified with Cernunnos of the Gauls. His heavy collar reminded me of those on certain figures of the lechs found in the Channel Islands, Brittany and France, and the conspicuous neck ornament and horn-like ears linked it to the god of the witches. Beside the 'cross' was another stone so deeply embedded as to be only just visible above the long grass. Graves overgrown with herbage obscured the outline of earthworks belonging to the Enclosure of the Synods, upon which the area of the churchyard had encroached.

Dusk was beginning to fall, but we did not want to leave before seeing the hill's two ancient springs, Caprach and Nemnach. Passing through the group of whitewashed houses, one or two with delightful flower gardens, we presently came to the first of these wells beside the lane, a stone canopy covering the water that flowed into a trough below. On the opposite side, half hidden by the wild growth of the hedge, was a small building which, we were told, was the first watermill in Ireland, though now in disuse. We talked to an old lady in one of the cottages about the spring, and she told us, disregarding its ancient name with complete confidence, that it was St Patrick's Well. It was now the chief water supply of the village.

Darkness was closing in, so we went no further in our search for Nemnach. The lane, the spring and the hamlet had an air of almost primeval quietude; the sides of Tara's hill, this gentle slope and the opposite wooded scarp, breathed a more highly charged atmosphere than the plateau at the top, though most of the antiquities were there. I could have spent many more hours wandering in the neighbourhood.

Five roads, as from Kells, once radiated from Tara; that by which we had come was anciently called Slighe Miodluachra and led northward through Navan to Emain Macha near Armagh. This, like Tara, was one of the four ancient royal palaces of Ireland. In the dark and wet we followed the modern road along the course of its predecessor and so regained Drogheda.

The Municipal
Gallery Visited

E VER SINCE READING two pieces in W.B. Yeats's *Last Poems*, 'Beautiful Lofty Things' and 'The Municipal Gallery Revisited', I was determined to see this collection of paintings. So, one damp afternoon, I found myself standing in Parnell Square and then passing through the Regency halls of Charlemont House until I reached Salon III, containing the Hugh Lane Bequest.

Immediately I forgot that I was looking at pictures at all; rather, I felt like a guest at some distinguished gathering surrounded, as so often in actuality, by the many one does not care about and the few who attract one at first glance. Perhaps this feeling was intensified because the collection was housed in a mansion where many receptions must have taken place. However this may be, all abstract consideration of aesthetics were forgotten, even the artists who painted these portraits sank almost into anonymity, their work seeming important only as a record of their sitters' character.

The one exception to this was the painting by Walt Kuhn of John Butler Yeats, father of the poet and the painter, who himself painted many of the well-known figures and influenced the style of Irish portraiture towards this very anonymity, this sinking of the artist in his sitter. Kuhn, on the other hand, had tried to dominate his subject; one felt that his main concern was not to render the personality of that domed head and loose-limbed body but to amuse himself by outlining their forms in ultramarine.

Perhaps an attitude neglectful of aesthetics is the best in any case for looking at portraits, unless a veritable masterpiece is under consideration, like Antonio Pollaiuolo's *Simonetta Vespucci*, or unless the subject is seen as generic, transcending the particular model, like Cézanne's *Old Woman with a Rosary*. Certainly, portraits should be arranged as they are here, unmixed with any other genre but linked by some social or historical theme.

Impelled by Yeats's poems to come here, I felt I was not only attending a reception but visiting the abode of Shades; and among the mighty dead I sought first the recorded likeness of my psychopomp. The scene of my only meeting with him in life was also an art exhibition in a large house, of which I was lucky enough to be in charge on the afternoon when he came to look around. I recognized him at once – a tall old man dressed in tweeds that recalled an autumnal mountain, silver hair flowing from under a wide black hat. Even today I remember many details of his appearance, how he supported himself on a stick, peering through glasses with tortoiseshell rims; he was wearing a green shirt, a white silk scarf and a ring of curious design.

I was struck by the glow of his skin – a clear orange colour, it seemed. He was very charming to me, though I was quite unknown at the time. He spoke as though in a light trance, almost automatically, and I could not follow all he said, but an unexpectedly robust humour flashed from time to time through his discourse. I realized that I had been too solemn in my previous reading of his works. He had a magnetic quality which I could not analyse but only feel; I wanted to follow him about wherever he went and, given any encouragement, would have done so.

Here I saw not the Yeats whom I remembered but Yeats

as a young man painted by his father. The dark face was turned away in perspective, as though the artist had been reluctant to show the full blaze of his son's personality. Already sensing his greatness, some envy must have arisen in him at its eclipsing force, so that he showed its vehicle as though itself in eclipse. One knows from the poet's *Autobiographies* of the tension between them at this time, though it was later resolved.

The next to catch my eye was Douglas Hyde, scholar and translator of poems from the Irish and first President of Éire. He wore the unbrushed hair that still seems to be the mode in this country, below which blue eyes shone brilliantly. Below these again grew a straggling moustache that is, fortunately, no longer fashionable.

Robert Gregory, a pretty boy of a type all too familiar in the art world, was shown dabbing at a canvas; one of his own decorative landscapes, of Coole Park, his home, hung in an adjoining salon. His mother, Lady Gregory, could only have been called Augusta. The ruling of inch-squares showed on Mancini's canvas in spite of the impasto of the paint, so that one seemed to be looking at the matriarch's face through a wire grille. But what immense Victorian dignity he built up there none the less!

Mahaffy's leonine head contrasted with Orpen's self-portrait, posed with a studied whimsicality. One shuddered as much at the display of self-consciousness as at the greensick tinging of the skin, rendered with a technique of nauseating slickness. I'm such a card, he was saying, I don't care how unattractive I am, you've got to take it – and what a humorous chap I am with it all!

And there was Edward Martyn, a plump capon whose pomposity was well conveyed; one understood from his face the projection of narcissism which flowered as an interest in choirboys. As at a social gathering, one gazed around wondering if, among much pretension, much of the mask, 'the sixty-year-old smiling public man', there was any face one could spontaneously admire or genuinely like. There were two, perhaps: that of Dr Mannix, ascetically fine drawn though much assisted by his ecclesiastical millinery; and that of Standish O'Grady, scholar and wit.

He looked straight out of his frame, grave and a little sad, with no attempt to hide or to dramatize himself. Sensitive without effeminacy, determined without rigour, the slate-blue eyes were bemused but unflinching, the slate-grey hair still rising thickly above the brow. Yet afterwards, when I saw other portraits of him in the National Gallery at Merrion Square, I grew doubtful, for there I had the impression of a character less satisfactory. In particular a pencil sketch, also by John B. Yeats, gave me a hint of something undirected, some deviation, which I would not have suspected from the large oil painting. What was the trouble – drink, perhaps?

> Standish O'Grady supporting himself between the tables
> Speaking to a drunken audience high nonsensical words –

Was this the record of some special occasion, or was it a scene that could have been witnessed almost any evening at some bar? However that may be, it was included by the poet among 'Beautiful Lofty Things'.

Shane Leslie was on the wall, too, looking rather like Gerald Yorke; and Sir Edward Carson, who might, by his features, have been a cousin of Oscar Wilde. Austin Stack, though represented as standing on a heathery hillside, looked like a dummy, due, no doubt, to reference from a photograph in the painting. He was a Republican, executed in the early days of the Free State; on the other side in 'the Troubles' and assassinated by the Republicans was Michael Collins, whose handsome mask, ennobled in death, was represented in the next room. A similar fate overtook Kevin O'Higgins; there was much subtlety in his glance, yet I would not have called him doom-eager but for Yeats's line:

A soul incapable of remorse or rest.

The martyrs of Easter 1916 were missing; Pearse and Connolly were among those 'sixteen dead men'. Joseph Plunkett, too – England, what have you done? I see his blood upon the Rose.

Though Lady Gregory dominated the women present, there were several others celebrated in their day. Hazel Lavery was painted as a beauty and no more, though she may have had hidden depths; Mrs Stephen Gwynn stared upwards with insolent ambition, an obvious go-getter; while Lady Beresford, handsome and healthy in an overblown way, played the fussy hostess. Of the Amazons, I searched in vain for Maud Gonne, as her portrait was on loan at the time; and the Countess Markievicz was shown not wearing the green uniform of her political heyday but in the sweeping ball dress of her early years, before she had outraged a conventional background. A drawing-room portrait in the manner of Sargent could give no impression of her strange character and destiny; sentenced to death for her part in the 1916 rebellion, she was two years later the first woman elected to the House of Commons, though, as a Sinn Féin member, she did not take her seat. But her portrait called to mind another of Yeats's poems, 'In Memory of Eva Gore-Booth and Con Markievicz', describing the two sisters as he had known them as a youth near Sligo:

both
Beautiful, one a gazelle.

How far from the 'gracious living' of Lissadell was her death, in 1927, in the public ward of a hospital! A portrait of 'Æ' by her husband Casimir was hanging in the same room.

But to me the most sympathetic was Jane Barlow, who wrote 'Lisnadara' among other now-almost-forgotten poems; surely it is to her picture that Yeats's lines refer:

> Before a woman's portrait suddenly I stand
> Beautiful and gentle in her Venetian way.
> I met her all but fifty years ago
> For twenty minutes in some studio.

Poor thing, she may have treasured that meeting, but with her fey look and delicate hands she would have been unable to give destiny a nudge and so did not speak to the busy man again. And it is easy to understand why Katherine Tynan Hinkson, a smug-faced, pink-and-ginger governess type, faded into the background of the poet's mind after his meeting with his muse:

> Maud Gonne at Howth station waiting a train,
> Pallas Athene in that straight back and arrogant head:

Finally, there was Augusta Gregory's nephew, Hugh Lane himself, pallid and Proustian, the host of this reception, to whom one owed not only Salon III but in large measure the foundation of the whole museum. Near by was the room reproachfully awaiting the return of 'the thirty-nine Lane Pictures', masterpieces of the modern French school which still repose in the keeping of the National Gallery, London. This room contained a list of the works in question with photographic reproductions, a copy of the codicil to Hugh Lane's will, a comment by Augustine Birrell, KC, on the British Government Committee of Inquiry into the matter and an extract from its findings.

The pictures were housed temporarily at the National Gallery, since no suitable accommodation could be found for them in Dublin at the time, but a codicil to the will left them to Dublin's Municipal Gallery. The codicil was, however, unwitnessed at the time of the testator's sudden death – he was drowned in the *Lusitania* – and was therefore held to be legally invalid. The authorities in London took advantage of this to retain the paintings, with the result that much rancorous controversy ensued, Yeats himself being one of the most strenuous campaigners for their return.

Justice and legality, though ideally synonymous, are not always so in fact, and justice, we are told, should not only be done but should also appear to be done. In this case, it appears not to have been done, since Hugh Lane's wishes were never in doubt. If the pictures were now given back, the gesture would do as much as any one thing could to promote good feeling between the two countries, for its repercussions would spread far beyond the confines of cultural circles.

Nothing in the Municipal Gallery impressed me more than the Lane Bequest, though the whole collection is worth studying. But some few works brought me a personal message, as, for instance, the mystic intensity of Simeon Solomon, represented by a painting, *The Finding of Moses*, and by several drawings. He remains the least-appreciated artist of those directly influenced by the Pre-Raphaelites, and his prose poems, too, are neglected. There were two exquisite Monticellis on view, *Forest Scene* and *The Banquet* – in few paintings can the fusing of theme and technique be so complete as here. In the first, the figures were part of the woodland, seeming to grow out of it as much as the trees – and this without crude metamorphosis, as of Syrinx into a reed or Daphne sprouting branches. The work expressed the intuition deep in many a myth, of the interchange of human life with that of vegetation. These figures came from humanity's dryad-stratum, existing in a leafy matrix; were they about to melt into the undergrowth, or had the surrounding woodland just put forth figures?

Of the bad painters, men are always worse than women, and here the two Henrys were an instance. Paul Henry's approach to the Irish scene was vulgar and insensitive; while Grace Henry, though not very competent, showed a genuine personal reaction.

I was struck, as always, by the marvellous colour of Jack Yeats; sometimes I think he is the only living colourist, certainly the only one these islands have produced. It was easy to compare *The Liffey Swim* and *The Maggie Man* with a still-life by Matthew Smith hanging near – how muddy and leaden his pigment seemed beside the luminous richness of Jack Yeats's! But his brother's poems had made Salon III for me the focus of the gallery. To know the personalities recorded there is to know an epoch of Irish social history – that germinal age from the 1880s to the 1930s during which the Gaelic revival produced a new movement in drama and letters, and Ireland became 'a nation once again'. Little is left of that brilliance in Dublin now, and those of younger generation show but dwarfishly in comparison with

All the Olympians; a thing never known again.